THERE'S ONLY ONE KEANO

MARK EVANS

First published in 1999 by
Marino Books
an imprint of Mercier Press
16 Hume Street Dublin 2
Tel: (01) 6615299; Fax: (01) 6618583
E.mail: books@marino.ie
Trade enquiries to CMD Distribution
55A Spruce Avenue
Stillorgan Industrial Park
email: cmd@columba.ie

The publishers are grateful to the following
for permission to reproduce copyright material:
Cobh Ramblers, Independent Newspapers,
INPHO and Sportsfile.

© Mark Evans 1999

ISBN 1 86023 098 9

10 9 8 7 6 5 4 3 2 1

A CIP record for this title is available from the British Library

Cover design by SPACE
Printed in Ireland by ColourBooks, Baldoyle Industrial Estate, Dublin 13

THERE'S ONLY ONE KEANO

ACKNOWLEDGEMENTS

Thanks to Paul Drury, *Evening Herald* editor;
Liam Mulcahy, *Evening Herald* photographic editor;
the sports departments, Independent Newspaper;
and special thanks to Frank Coughlan.

To Veronica, in the premier league of wives . . .

CONTENTS

INTRODUCTION

Roy Keane came into the world on 10 August 1971 – a time of decline for Manchester United. Four days after Roy's birth in Cork, the bulk of the European Cup-winning team of 1968 was still in the first team, but the glory days were firmly in the past. Household names like George Best, Denis Law, Bobby Charlton, Brian Kidd, Alex Stepney and Tony Dunne started the first game of the new season – away to Derby County – four days after Roy's birthday, drew 2-2, and came a disappointing eighth in the First Division.

A generation later, Roy would power the team to only its second-ever European Cup final.

Those who have known him remark on the one quality – determination – that has taken him from the small Cork suburb of Mayfield on to the world stage. Despite the best efforts of some British tabloids to paint a rough, tough upbringing, Roy has always stayed true to his roots, maintaining that he is from Cork first, Ireland second. The area of Mayfield is close-knit, but a lot quieter and more affluent than the reports would have us believe. And despite his hard man image, the player is proud to reveal a happy childhood.

Soccer was always a passion for generations on mother Marie's and dad Mossie's sides of the family. In the present generation, Roy's brothers Denis, Pat and Johnson have all impressed at various levels, while

Marie's father and two brothers won FAI medals.

Teachers at St John's Primary and Mayfield Community school remember Roy as a quiet, likeable kid, but one who was always more at home on the pitch than in the classroom. Soccer has always been a passion – Roy admits to being 'Spurs-mad' as a youth – but sports of all codes were part of his life. Famously, Keane boxed four times – and won all four times in the Mayfield tournament in the Irish Novice League. 'He was always very jolly, very respectful, a really good boy,' remembers Breda Lynch of the Brian Dillon Boxing Club, where the pre-teen Roy trained.

But boxing fans also recall one thing about Roy – his size. 'He was a good enough build, but he was a small kid,' one remembers. At soccer, lack of height would also prove a hindrance to his early career.

Setbacks are nothing new to Roy, and the player courted at times by clubs all over England, Spain and Italy has had his ups and downs. 1999 has been no exception: from the glory of the header against Juventus to the bitter disappointment of missing the Barcelona final. At international level, he has commanded games, inspired Ireland's best performances at the '94 Cup, but at other times has been criticised over his commitment to the cause.

Amazingly, Roy Keane did not win any awards for an awe-inspiring season at Old Trafford, but he undoubtedly has the respect of his peers. Republic of Ireland midfield partner, the Charlton Athletic star Mark Kinsella, sums up the feelings of many Premiership players: 'It's always tough against Roy . . . always. It was nervewracking the first time I played alongside him for Ireland, but he's a great midfield partner. At Charlton, we've watched him to learn ideas from the man who is probably the top midfield player in Britain.'

But it hasn't been a rapid rise to the top – the road to Barcelona took 21 years from Communion age at Cork's Rockmount club, through to League of Ireland, triumph and tragedy at Forest, and trophies and injuries at the world's biggest club – Manchester United . . .

'I CALLED HIM THE BOILERMAN.'

Roy Keane's football career began far from the adoring tens of thousands of fans at Old Trafford, or the baying crowds of rival fans at the likes of Elland Road or Anfield. Roy scored his first goals, harried defenders and ran midfields on Cork's northside in the early to mid-1980s with Rockmount AFC, now 75 years in existence. His brothers, Denis and Johnson, had played for the club and his uncle Michael Lynch was a manager. His manager at junior level, Tim Murphy, remembers a player who sounds eerily like the present midfield dynamo. 'I called him the boilerman,' says Murphy, 'because he'd run all day and would hate to lose a match.' The professional, never-say-die Man United spirit was with him from the very start, too. 'Once, he gave a bad back pass to the keeper, and the opposition got in to score a goal. The next thing, he got the ball and ran through their defence and scored – he wouldn't want to be seen to let the side down.'

Murphy was the first of many coaches to recognise Keano's dedication to the bane of many a footballer's life – preparation. 'He was excellent at training,' says Murphy. 'Come hail, rain or snow he'd come out. The lad would train in the morning and after tea if he could.' Again, like others, the manager realised that Keane could run rings around older – and bigger – opposition. 'He'd always hold his own on the park against older lads. He'd be under 13 but would be playing the under-14s,' says Murphy. 'He could be battered by centre-forwards or whatever but was never injured. He would never complain and would take the knocks.' He was such a prospect that he scooped the club's Under-11 Player of the Year Award – at the tender age of nine and a half! But Murphy adds that height was a hassle. 'The scouts from England were looking for height and muscle but despite that, Roy had impeccable timing in his heading of the ball.'

Nowadays the emphasis in football has largely shifted to skill rather than brawn, but in the 1980s the long ball game and aggression dominated more in English football. 'Roy plays a great game,' Murphy believes. 'He protects the back four and plays the simple pass if that's what's needed. What he doesn't do is give the ball away easily. But at that time, as he was being overlooked, he was getting restless as others went over to England.' As Roy hit his late teens, other team-mates had already gone across the water. Paul McCarthy had opted for Brighton, while Alan O'Sullivan had left for Luton, all in the space of a few months.

The present chairman of Rockmount, John Delay, was Roy's assistant manager at senior level, from 16 upwards. He remembers a player who was 'mad for it, mad for the game of football'.

'His enthusiasm for the game was always the same, from the first to the ninetieth minute; it was the same commitment,' says John Delay. He recounts a great tradition of football in the family. 'Denis Keane was a marvellous player – and in the 15–18 age group he was as good, if not better, than Roy. He was a great box-to-box player too, at the left side of midfield.' Roy's great asset, apart from skill, was his commitment, he feels. 'He was over-enthusiastic at times,' Delay remembers. 'He'd want to play a minor game at two, a senior game at six, and then go training afterwards!'

The late eighties were a golden period for the Whitechurch-based club, which is again enjoying success a decade later. 'Roy was part of a great team,' says Delay. 'About five of them were in the Cork team that won the Kennedy Cup.' He adds, 'Roy was smaller than the likes of Len Downey and Paul McCarthy, but he was a little nipper who got past people.'

Interest in Keane was brewing back home, with Cork City and Cobh Ramblers both keen to sign him. Delay was sad to see his precious player leave but accepts that 'he might not have got his big break without it. It put him in the shop window, the League of Ireland.' And the northside of Cork, and Rockmount people, where the team won the double for six years, are proud of his achievements. 'I was watching the Barcelona final in my local pub,' says Delay, who regularly visits Roy at Old Trafford. 'It was a great win for his family, for Rockmount and for Cork. It's just such a pity he could not have lifted the cup as a player.'

2

'THIS COULD BE YOUR DAY, KID, YOU NEVER KNOW.'

Eddie O'Rourke is well-known in the close-knit island community of Cobh, 15 miles away from Cork city via a single bridge. The O'Rourke family is inextricably linked with local club Cobh Ramblers, founded in 1922. Eddie's brother John O'Rourke is the chairman of the club, while nephew John is the current manager. Lifelong Manchester United fan Eddie has to put up with the jokes of ABUs (the Anyone But United brigade) in local pubs if the Reds lose a game and is instantly recognisable on the highways and byways of the area 'because of the old car' – a 1983 Fiat 127 that has seen better days. But Eddie always has the last laugh, because he is the man who brought Roy Keane to national prominence, with Cobh Ramblers' youth team. Always on the lookout for great young footballing talent, he struck gold with Roy, who he signed from Rockmount. 'You never know what will happen with the younger players,' says the former youth manager. 'Little did I know when I was in the dressing room, talking to him about different things, that he'd be captain of Manchester United, captain of Ireland.'

'The way I remember him always, though, is waiting outside Fitzpatrick's Hotel in Wilton in all weather for the lift to training or matches. I'd seen him before, as I used to go around and I'd look at many players. My job was, like, not only the youth team but to see beyond that – whether he would go straight up to the senior team – which five or six of them from that youth team did. At the moment there's three from that team still playing with the first team. They all hung around with Roy.'

He remembers the fateful day he signed the young Keane for Cobh, at a time when there was considerable interest shown in him by local rivals Cork City. 'I just said, "Would you like to come down and play for Cobh youths? It's a stepping stone for League of Ireland. And you never know," I said, "what could come out of it."'

O'Rourke believes that he was blessed: 'The story is that the price of a stamp cost his registration fee. When I came down to Cobh I said, "I've got this guy from Rockmount called Roy Keane; you've to sign him; he's the best I've ever seen, by a mile." City were probably looking as well. Our secretary got the registration form away first and Cork City's was later – they say they hadn't a stamp ready at the time and Cobh's reached the FAI office first.'

Eddie O'Rourke remembers a player with a professional approach, even in the hard-tackling world of youth and League of Ireland football: 'He'd never kick the wall or the dressing-room door over losing, he'd just take it along with the winning,' and he is convinced that hasn't changed over the years. 'I know that he was bitterly disappointed to be out of the Barcelona game, but he just shrugs it off and says, "What can we do?" Roy's private – he probably did his own crying inside, as his attitude was always, "We did our best, we can do no more." And people don't realise he's not dirty but he's very competitive all the time.'

Roy developed more and more as a player at Ballyleary training ground, a field not far from the club's St Coleman's Park ground, and was an instant hit. Eddie O'Rourke remembers: 'I saw him one day, then he had to go to Limerick for a replay but I signed him then and brought him down and put him into the reserve team, but I knew that he wasn't going to be there for long as he was just a colossus on the youth team. I said to first-team coach Liam McMahon, "You'll have to put him into the reserves and the first team."'

At Cobh, Roy's team won everything – except the FAI Cup – at youth level. 'I never in my life saw anyone who could run from box to box like him,' says O'Rourke, 'and his jumping was unreal. His timing . . . they'd all be jumping up in a game and you'd see this fella. Like a salmon he'd just soar up with perfect timing. He was a good goal-scorer at Forest but, funny enough, he wasn't so much for us. He was always there to stop them from scoring. They'd be just about to do it and he'd nick in and take it and set us up again. He got one or two goals for us all right.'

He adds, 'It was always in the middle of the park that we'd play him but your man's engine was unreal – he could play anywhere. There were times there that he'd be attacking one minute from a corner – he'd be up for that – the next minute he'd be down in the other box taking the ball away, starting us up again.'

And he reckons it was Keane's driving ambition which turned him into the professional he is today: 'We sent him on a FÁS course with a guy called Darren Fenton who had great ability but not Keane's mentality, because Keane would go through anything to get what he wanted. He really wanted to get to the top.' He adds that getting there hasn't changed Keane, who still pays many visits to his home town of Cork: 'There's no rubbish out of him, he just talks straight out and gives you the picture as he sees it.'

The new sports coaching and management course for young footballers, run by state training agency FÁS, was directed by Maurice Price, who was assisted by Larry O'Mahony. Participants spend up to 18 months on the scheme, and over 500 players have passed through the course since it started in 1989.

'That course had 24 young lads, aged 16 to 18 years,' says Price. 'They were all League of Ireland – Cobh, Waterford, Donegal, Limerick and so on. But the same old problem – size – cropped up yet again. The thing about Roy is that when he was younger he was a bit small for his age. He never got into the young international teams – maybe because of his height.'

But what he lacked in inches he made up for in effort. 'He always had a go,' Price remembers about Keano's performance on the pitch. 'And he was always confident in what he did. I always remember that he was in training – and he had a good attendance. He wanted to make it, and I knew he'd do well.'

Spending the week in digs away from home was a tough experience for many of the youngsters, and Roy was no exception. 'At first he was shy – he'd kick himself a lot if something went wrong on the pitch – but the lads were all the same at first. The first few months are difficult, then they gel as a squad.'

Keane's teenage years were a time of frustration as he watched other youngsters heading off to big-name English clubs. But Price feels that going to England at age 14 or 15 could have been disastrous for Keane. 'He developed late and I think most players who do well in England develop late. The course has a high standard and nearly all on it made it to League of Ireland at least. When kids go to England at 14, they end up in strange cities like Birmingham. But the problem is that they're getting homesick and not getting full-time training. There's no league at 14, so they can't do too much. In Ireland they can still play schoolboys' league.'

At the course, Keane was getting the kind of training that would stand him in good stead at Cobh Ramblers and later at Nottingham Forest. 'When he went to Forest, he went there very fit,' says Price. 'On the course, it was five days a week of effort. On a typical day you'd start with warm-ups and developing your touch. Then you'd move on to three versus three games, learn about shooting, midfield play, then have a few talks. We went to the

VEC [local school] on Tuesday afternoons, and the lads would learn a new language or how to fill out forms. It wasn't all on the field – even if that's what the players wanted!'

But one former team-mate reveals that Roy's attitude made him stand out: 'He was not attending classes as much as he should have. But he said to me, "Classes are not important; I'll be a success." Now that's what I call confidence.'

And the same problems at Rockmount AFC and at the course continued to dog the ambitious young player at club level in Cobh. 'I often had a conversation with him. We'd sit down and he'd ask me, "Will I ever make it?" There was fellas going over there [to England] at 14 or 15,' says Eddie O'Rourke, but adds that he told Roy that heading away at a young age was not necessarily the break he'd been desperately seeking. 'It's all wrong,' he feels, 'they should be left till they're 18 and they'll know what's ahead of them. This fella was going, that fella was going – from all angles. Of course I could see it. Naturally enough, he was probably saying to himself, "What's wrong with me, why amn't I going?" and I used to say to him all the time, "Roy, your day will come, and you're at the right age." Well, I didn't know that we were going to have the success that we had because we won everything to be won that year – bar the FAI Cup.'

'He was very shy, very quiet,' Eddie O'Rourke remembers. 'There's a picture of him in Rockmount: all around him were going on trials and the Irish teams weren't picking him, but then again the Dubs were biased then! He was playing down in Cork and they'd be sending up reports, and I suppose they were saying he was too small, saying he was this and he was that. In those days you'd have to be a big man to play in England. But look at him now – he's towering now and look at the legs on him.'

Even before that time, a 15-year-old Roy was so desperate for success in England that he had written to all 92 league clubs there. Few wrote back, but a certain Brian Clough did, explaining that if he was ambitious enough, his talent would shine through.

O'Rourke recalls the day Roy began his move towards First Division football in England with Brian Clough's Nottingham Forest. 'Although we didn't win the FAI Cup, the irony is that because of it Roy got to be seen in Dublin against Belvedere. He used to say to me how it was an amazing thing how he was discovered. I'm amazed that they [football scouts] didn't see him. Not knocking the Dubs, but the scouts only go around the Dublin parks. They think that's where the talent is, but the talent is everywhere.'

He recalls the background to the fateful game against Belvedere in the football heartland of Fairview Park on the northside of Dublin, a mine of talent for hunting scouts. 'With Belvedere everything was going to clockwork. A fella put a ball in and it came in from the left – I can still see it today – and Keane dived at it, 1-0.' However, Cobh later got caught for a goal in the last minute of the game, and the club faced a tough task away in Dublin, on 18 February 1990. After a gruelling game, Roy would have to play with the first team, up in Ballybofey against Finn Harps.

'I often think to myself if we'd won it 1-0 we'd probably have gone on to win the thing but they all say, "Would he have been seen?" But sure Jesus he'd have to be seen because at that time he was breaking into the first team and he was up at Coleman's Park in the League of Ireland First Division. His performances were unbelievable.' But the away leg to Belvedere, which was nothing short of disastrous, turned Roy's career. 'We were getting the bus up to play Belvedere in Dublin and he says to me, "Will I ever make it?" And I just said, "This could be your day, kid, you never know." Honestly, it was just the normal thing to say. It was his day, wasn't it, and he was made then.'

But it didn't seem that way a couple of hours later: 'We were hammered that day because the preparations were all at fault – we were hammered, hammered,' Eddie O'Rourke remembers. 'We were just not tuned in on the day. The bus was late, we were late togging off, everything went wrong but we didn't deserve to get hammered on the day. Roy was head and shoulders above everything out there, even though we were beaten 4-0.'

The Cobh manager wasn't the only one to believe that Roy had tremendous potential. 'What really caught me about him in Fairview Park that morning was the fact that he could take on players at ease,' recalls the former Nottingham Forest scout, Dubliner Noel McCabe. 'He'd just go by them; he was great at getting to the back line and getting balls over – he did that three or four times in the game. But the biggest thing of all, I suppose, was his heading ability – it was absolutely brilliant. He was only 5' 11", if he was that, but he was absolutely marvellous in the air, getting up, and he was a big strong boy, obviously from training. He had ability, great ability.'

O'Rourke remembers: 'Your man Noel McCabe came in to the park on his little bike and over he went to us – fair play to McCabe, he was on the ball.' Eddie's brother John O'Rourke, the club chairman, recalls his first meeting with the scout. 'He came over to me at half-time, and he was originally interested in a player called Jamie Culliemore. But he asked, "Who is this No 10?" and I told him he was Roy Keane.'

'We were over the road in a pub having sandwiches,' Eddie says, 'and McCabe was the only one who came in for the meal. I'd often ask myself what all the others were looking at. I could have rung someone before that, but that's not my job: I'm a scout for Cobh Ramblers. But I could have gotten on to someone from United about him. I'd say he [McCabe] saw Keane previous to that in Cork. I have an awful feeling we played a crowd called Wilton in Cork previous to that time and we beat Wilton – one of the top sides in Cork around that time – and we beat them 3-1. Keane was immaculate in that game.'

Noel McCabe reveals that he had already been on Roy's trail before the Dublin tie: 'George Scannell, from the Casement Club in Cork, told me about him,' he says, and he witnessed Roy in action for Rockmount against Belvedere Boys in an FAI Youth Cup tie in 1988. 'Right from the start I knew that here was a very special talent and I kept up my interest when the lad signed for Cobh Ramblers. I went up to see him play for Cobh in a League of Ireland game when he was only 17 and he wasn't playing, he was only starting there, it was against Home Farm in Tolka Park. I had seen him under-14 about three years prior to that, and he was small and wasn't the best player on the park; the best player went was another boy [Alan O'Sullivan], who went to Luton. Roy Keane didn't go on trial at all that year. I approached Cobh after the match and said, "Look I'd like to talk to the boy" with a view to taking him to Forest for a trial. John O'Rourke said to give me a ring tomorrow and I'll see him as he's on a FÁS course here in Dublin out in Stewart's Hospital.'

But other scouts who had seen Roy play at less than his peak were not impressed. 'Interest from other scouts? None, none at all,' says Noel McCabe about that day in Fairview Park.

The events of the weeks to come put Roy on to one of the biggest stages in football.

3

'He Went Home A Boy, Came Back A Man.'

Scout Noel McCabe was keen to get Roy off to Nottingham for a trial, and his scouting report records: 'Roy is a player who in this game showed me he has good skill and vision in finding players with his passes. He is aggressive with his tackling and was involved in all activity around the middle of the park. His pace is very good and he loved taking on players and going for the back line and could get good crosses in. He looks a nice balanced player and his upper body is broad and appears a very strong-looking boy. He is, in my opinion, a player to go on trial to Forest right away.'

After the meeting with Cobh Ramblers, McCabe got on the trail of this new prospect in Dublin. 'The next morning I called the boy and we met in the Ashling Hotel beside Heuston Station.'

He was 'very shy', McCabe remembers, 'I was doing all the talking.' But he adds, 'He was desperate to get away. It was a big thing to get on trial, as it still is. I travel a lot, and the boys are over-anxious to get away. He was at a very good age, going on 19, and had never been capped at senior level. He was mature, and he had been away from home on the FÁS course so he was getting into that scheme of things, training full time on the course.

'Forest was a great club to go to. It had the European

Cup record, a great ground and a lovely city.' However, the aspiring young star who had dashed off dozens of letters to clubs in England was still unsure about how to further his career. 'It was a new ball game; he gave the impression that he was looking forward to it but didn't know what to expect. Like with most good players, I was doing the talking for him.'

'He went over for a week,' he recalls, and made an immediate impression on veteran manager Brian Clough's ambitious club with its proud history as double European Cup winners.

'He was due back on the Sunday morning to play for Cobh, but I got a phone call on the Saturday evening from assistant manager Ronnie Fenton. The first team had been playing QPR in London and they got back on the Saturday evening. They said the boy Keane was probably back as Cobh needed him for the match. He couldn't get a flight so he got a flight to Dublin and a train down to Cork,' McCabe remembers. "We want him back," they said. It was because Archie Gemmill liked him a lot. They didn't see him in action as they had left on Friday for London for the match, so they missed him at a critical time, so they got him back.'

'You could see that he was going to go places and it was only a matter of time; I was delighted for him,' says Eddie O'Rourke. 'He went at the right time. Say that he went to Manchester United or Liverpool; he would have come through, but he went to a Forest side that were playing football that suited him. He had the right man in charge of him.'

Dealing with a major English club at this level was a daunting new experience for Cobh, John O'Rourke remembers. 'Myself and John Meade, our secretary, went over, but we brought former Chelsea and Cobh player John Hollins, now manager of Swansea City, as he played one game for us in the past, and we needed someone with experience of England. We dealt with assistant manager Ronnie Fenton from the start, but we couldn't come to an agreement on the money. We wanted 20 grand up front; but he offered us only ten. We had hit a stalemate, and then Clough comes in. He shook all our hands and offered us all a drink, which we all took – well, I did anyway – and he started talking to Fenton. As if he didn't know how good Roy was, he asked, "Is he any good, then?" and Ronnie said he could be very good. He then asked, "What's the problem?" And we then came to agreement. He had even kissed me on the head when he came in the door.' But, he recalls, 'he was only with us ten minutes, and the deal was done. We felt it was a bit of a ploy.'

By today's standards, the money doesn't seem much, but Cobh were relatively happy with the £47,000 they made from the Keane deal, even though it came in dribs and drabs. 'We got £20,000 up front, then there were two stages of £10,000 each – the first for his first ten first-team games, the second for the next ten – then the final payment, of £7,000, was for his first five international caps. We also got a game in Cobh, and Forest came over with the likes of Stuart Pearce as part of the deal.'

But Roy was to be sold by Forest to Manchester United in the space of three years, with Cobh not receiving a penny from the deal. 'That was the unfortunate part,' says O'Rourke. 'We had no knock-on clause, and that was the most regrettable thing, but at the time our big concern was the up-front money. When I think of the value of him today . . . 47 grand is peanuts, but it was very good for us at the time.' And he's sanguine about the dealings, saying, 'I have no regrets; sooner or later some other club would have come in for him. I'm just amazed that only Forest did, even though there were rumours about Spurs and Brighton showing an interest.'

Keane has been the biggest find so far by McCabe, who now scouts for the prestigious Liverpool Academy, run by Steve Heighway. But the reward for the find was not the windfall many would have expected. 'I received £500 for him signing pro and then, when he made the first team, I got £1,000.' But he's not complaining about the amount: 'It's nice to be rewarded, as many in this town are in schoolboy football on a voluntary basis.' And he adds, 'It's just part of the job; I have two boys now over at Liverpool, and that's what it's about. And I have four others on Liverpool's books. This [Ireland] is a hotbed of talent. There were only about four or five of us scouting at that stage, but it's boomed now.' And Eddie O'Rourke remembers: 'After Keane was hooked they were over in droves in this town, all the scouts, but the horse had gone, bolted!'

Forest were delighted with their latest acquisition, and, as one club source maintains, 'Forest saw Roy Keane as one of the best bits of business they have ever done. They paid just £47,000 for him and sold him for £3.75 million. And there was also the bonus of getting two good seasons out of him.' Roy's rise to footballing riches at the City Ground was nothing short of meteoric. 'He was always known as the lad who came from nowhere; that impressed fans more than anything, to go on to one of the biggest stages in football. On his away debut, Cloughie had to introduce him to his team-mates!' says the club source.

But many people at the City Ground could see the massive potential of this 'boy from nowhere' who had risen from £35-a-week part-timer to £3,000-a-week star. 'When it came to training, he was one who came in and got on with his job. He was the typical guy next door in many ways, but he came out as he established himself as a force,' says one backroom source. 'Before, it was like talking to an adolescent schoolboy, meek and mild, who needed to develop parts of his game. But from the start he knew he was something special, and he was very confident for an 18-year-old.'

After just ten minutes of reserve-team football, Keane got his chance to shine in the English First Division – away to Liverpool, of all teams. Facing the Merseyside giants – who were chasing after another Championship to add to a long list of trophies – was a tall order, even for a lad with Roy's confidence.

'I had a phone call from the manager on the morning of the game to my digs in Nottingham and he told me to bring my boots with me – but there was never a hint that he was going to play me in the match,' Keane said at the time. Brian Clough only informed him of the decision to play him 50 minutes before kick-off, as he was putting out the kit. 'Irishman, what are you doing?' Clough was said to have asked.

'Putting the gear out, boss,' Keane answered.

'Son, put the No 7 shirt on, you're playing,' came the reply.

Keane was said to have gone momentarily pale at the thought, but he says, 'I grabbed the chance.'

Back home, there was even greater shock, as John O'Rourke remembers: 'His father phoned me that night and said, "Roy is heading up to Anfield: the reserves must be playing." I said, "No, it's the first team," and he couldn't believe it.'

And the Cobh man is still impressed with 'old big 'ead's style of management. 'I think he was a marvel with the youths. Roy in Anfield . . . after just a month. I don't think any other club would have given him the break.'

But no one was more shocked than the 19-year-old himself. 'I couldn't believe it when I found out that I was going to play in the first match and everything since then has been a dream. I thought I was only going along for the experience. But, although we lost, the other lads helped me tremendously and I have been lucky enough to keep my place.'

A STAR IS BORN: Roy, in 1991, setting out on the path of an international career.
© INPHO

RAMBLER ROY: Back at St Coleman's Park with Eddie O'Rourke before the move to Forest.
© Cobh Ramblers

BOY DONE GOOD: Forest player Roy back at home to accept the Munster Cup.
L-R: Cobh Chairman John O'Rourke, Roy, Eddie O'Rourke and Pat O'Mahony of the local council.
© Cobh Ramblers

Local Hero: Chatting with supporters at Cobh Ramblers, aged just 17.
© Cobh Ramblers

He's a Star: Roy was a huge hit with fans at Forest, United and the Republic.
© Independent Newspapers

CITY SLICKER: Roy impressed for Nottingham Forest at home in the City Ground and away during the 1993 season.
© INPHO

RED-HOT AGAINST CHILE: Roy Keane makes his senior debut against Chile at Lansdowne Road on May 22, 1991.
© Sportsfile

TEEN KEANE: Proudly wearing the Irish strip in 1990. © Independent Newspapers

BATTLER: In action for Republic, 1990. © Independent Newspapers

YOUNG GUN: Roy quickly impresses at senior level for the Republic.
© INPHO

FAMILY FORTUNES: Brother Pat Keane, playing for Cobh Ramblers, is tackled by Sean Mulhall of Garda AFC in the Harp Lager Senior Challenge Cup in January 1999.
© Sportsfile

COMING ON IN LEAPS: In action against
Poland in 1991, the Irishman was a
firm favourite with Brian Clough
at Nottingham Forest.
© Independent Newspapers

RAPID RISE: The Corkman developed quickly
on the club and international scene in the
early nineties.
© Independent Newspapers

LEFT FOR DEAD: Taking international football by storm.
© Independent Newspapers

FANS' FAVOURITE: Taking time out after training to sign autographs.
© Independent Newspapers

GREEN MACHINE: Roy playing for Ireland's youth team.
© Independent Newspapers

SALUTING THE CROWD: Roy's Senior debut
against Chile.
© Independent Newspapers

MAN OF THE MOMENT: Winning the
FAI/Opel Young Player of the
Year award in 1991.
© Independent Newspapers

Hot News: Contemplates move to Manchester giants.
© Independent Newspapers

The Full-Back: Keano training
at Clonshaugh with Ireland's
Mick Byrne.
© Independent Newspapers

On a High: Ireland power their way to USA '94.
© Independent Newspapers

SIZING UP THE OPPOSITION: Roy lining out for the Republic of Ireland v. Macedonia in the 1997 World Cup Qualifier away in Skopje.
© INPHO

WOUNDED PRIDE: Roy in Dublin for sponsors Diadora during his long absence from action due to his ligament injury.
© SPORTSFILE

GRAFTER: Preparation has been a feature of Roy's game from
the early days to the present.
© Independent Newspapers

Later, a key role as midfielder for the Republic of Ireland Youths Championship in Hungary also helped his progress. 'We trained very hard, and I was fighting fit when I arrived at the City Ground. A couple of injuries and I was in – incredible,' said the Ireland under-21 skipper, who had only made his under-21 debut in October 1990, against Turkey in Dublin's Dalymount Park. Clough revealed to the *Daily Express* at the time: 'You didn't have to be a genius to see that he had something going for him – even my wife could have spotted it. He's one of the best headers of a ball I've come across. Blow me, I've not seen anyone jump so well since Red Rum called it a day.'

'His home debut was against Southampton, on September 8, and I was there for it,' says Noel McCabe. Also getting a glimpse of the big-time football action were Roy's parents, Marie and Mossie, and two of his brothers. 'There was a scouts' meeting on the Friday night and they were saying that they were looking forward to seeing him play a home game,' says McCabe. They weren't disappointed, and Keane left the field to a standing ovation from the Forest faithful. Although Roy's stint at Anfield was initially a stop-gap measure, because of injury to Steve Hodge, the Corkman became a permanent face on the first team and played against Coventry City after the Anfield encounter. 'They were using him in certain areas – like goal kicks from the keeper were to be directed at Roy Keane because of his excellent heading ability. Little things like that the manager had pointed out at team talks,' says McCabe, adding: 'The biggest thing they thought about Roy was that they could play him anywhere. He could score goals, had great anticipation and was great on the channels.'

And no less a figure than Cloughie realised that Roy not only had potential but was capable of looking after himself from Highbury to Hillsborough. 'He might only be 19 and a total stranger to the First Division, but you would think he had been playing there all his life,' said Clough, adding that he had even benefited veteran defender Stuart Pearce. 'He made Stuart Pearce's job so easy for him. I bet Pearcy was wishing he could have put him in his bag and taken him down to Wembley for England's tie against Hungary!'

And Roy had mutual respect for the gaffer. After his move to Old Trafford in 1993, he revealed: 'Brian Clough will always be the man responsible for giving me the chance to take on the footballing world. From the day I arrived at the City Ground, he took an interest in me and was always brilliant towards me. I can honestly say that I would not be the player I am today if it hadn't been for him.'

At Forest, Keane helped guide the team – who, in 1990, had won the last Littlewood's Cup final – to the 1991 FA Cup final. 'They were brilliant to look at in the early nineties,' McCabe remembers. 'He was brought on by a good man who loved his football and they played to their strengths. They had this marvellous thing where he'd make runs from the half-way line into the penalty area, and the ball would automatically come up to him. He was devastating like that.' But the manager was not always delighted with Roy's on-the-field antics. After scoring a goal against big boys Norwich City, he executed a perfect somersault for the fans. Clough threatened to sell him to a circus if he ever tried to repeat the feat. But he could always forgive the kind of star who would play a stormer in the 4-0 crushing of West Ham in the FA Cup semi-final.

Forest's exciting young side faced Tottenham at Wembley, but Keane was also getting rave reviews elsewhere. He was just pipped to the post for the prestigious Young Eagle of the Year Award – an award he was to win the following year – by Manchester United winger Lee Sharpe. The panel of England team manager Graham Taylor, Irish boss Jack Charlton and soccer names Jimmy Armfield, Ron Greenwood, Bill Nicholson, Stan Cullis, Trevor Cherry and Terry Yorath had to choose the most exciting young player in English soccer. 'Roy Keane is an exceptionally good player but what probably edges it for me is Lee Sharpe's ability to cope mentally with the demands of playing for a big club,' said Taylor. But the England manager paid tribute to the 21-year-old the following year: 'Jack Charlton is a very lucky man to have Keane. Not only is he good from box to box and an excellent passer of the ball, he also knows how to intercept and tackle; he scores more than his quota of goals. In fact, I don't think you could ask much more of a player as young as him.' But Keane's mind was on 18 May and recovering from a knock to his calf in time to tackle Terry Venables's Spurs side, which included such superstars as Gary Lineker and Paul Gascoigne.

'It's nice to have everyone available [for the final],' assistant manager Ron Fenton said at the time. 'Roy was our only doubt and had he not got through 90 minutes in the reserves the other night he would not have been on the team coach.'

'All the time I was sitting around seeing the days pass by and I wondered if I'd make it. It was agony waiting to get a match in. When I knew that I was playing on Tuesday, I also realised it was going to be all or nothing. If I had not come through that match without trouble, then my chance of a place at Wembley would have been zero,' Roy remembers.

The following Friday, Roy was on the team bus to the Twin Towers. Fully fit, he was a sure starter after Brian Clough admitted that, along with Stuart Pearce, Roy had kept the club motoring along earlier in the season. 'I'm not forgetting that easily,' he said. Indeed, Roy kept veteran England international Steve Hodge out of the side. Clough had been so impressed with Keane's versatility that, after he had played as a stand-in centre-half, the manager compared him to the great Franz Beckenbauer.

The admiration was mutual. Roy says that after Clough's departure, 'I got on very well with Brian. It baffled me the way some of the established stars at Forest got into a panic every time he was around the place. I was never afraid of him. I got on with him and if he said something I disagreed with, I'd tell him. He was a very nice man most of the time and was especially charming when he met my mother and father.'

The irony was that Roy's biggest moment was coming against the team he adored as a child. 'I was a big Spurs fan when I was a kid and when I watched them on television it was always in the back of my mind that I would love to play for them. Now all I am looking forward to is trying to beat them!'

One man proudly watching as Roy walked out on to the Wembley turf was Cobh's John O'Rourke. 'The amazing thing was, with all the stars out there, they were kind of depending on Roy to win it for them,' he believes. 'I remembered back to one of his last games for us, a cup game against Monaghan United, and he still gave everything. I can honestly say that I have never seen him play a bad game.'

The FA Cup final of '91 will always be remembered for Paul Gascoigne's over-the-top challenge on Gary Charles and Charles's horrific cruciate ligament injury. But after Stuart Pearce put Forest ahead in the first half, Paul Stewart equalised in the second and a Des Walker own goal settled the tie for the Londoners.

Despite the defeat, Roy's first season had been a revelation, and the following two seasons were, to say the least, eventful. By the end of the '91–'92 season, he was to appear in two Wembley finals and make his senior international debut, against Chile at Lansdowne Road on 22 May. And the youngster was to score eight goals – not bad at all for a midfielder in a mid-table side. Before the start of the season, Roy's manager felt that he needed to build himself up to withstand more seasons playing midfield at top-division football. 'Cloughie sent him home and put him on a diet of Guinness to fill him out during the summer,' says a Forest backroom source. 'He went home a boy, came back a man and was as well-built as a brick shithouse.'

The new season saw the arrival of a player Roy would get to know even better in later years: striker Teddy Sheringham. From the off, the £2 million Millwall man made an impact, setting up and scoring goals. In only the fifth game of the season, the young side, containing such players as Nigel Clough, Gary Charles, new signing Teddy Sheringham and Kingsley Black and, of course, Keane, were clicking as a unit. In the fifth game of the season – against Oldham Athletic – Keane was perfectly set up by Nigel Jenson to score in the 3-1 win at the City Ground. And by 7 September, Sheringham was regularly carving open defences, doing so yet again for Roy Keane in a game against Sheffield Wednesday. Keane was perfectly set up by the Londoner, but his effort was saved by on-form international keeper Chris Woods. A week later, Keane overwhelmed Wimbledon with a first-class display of football, boosting his side to eighth in the table. After the visitors went ahead in the second minute, Keane took control, equalising nine minutes later. A Kingsley Black goal put the home side 2-1 ahead, only for Keane to score again two minutes after the restart in the 4-2 demolition of the Dons.

But Forest, despite an abundance of young talent, was still a mid-table side. However, it was a force to be reckoned with at cup level. By March 1992, Nottingham Forest was back at Wembley, against Southampton. In the proud old stadium, Roy lifted his first of many cups, after his side won the Zenith Data Systems Cup final. A month later, the club returned to the Twin Towers, in the Rumbelows Cup final against Manchester United, who had beaten Cambridge, Portsmouth, Oldham, Leeds United and Middlesbrough to reach the last stage of the competition.

'Roy played a key role in getting Forest to the League Cup final in 1992,' remembers one Forest veteran. 'He scored a vital goal against Tottenham in the semi-final when we thought we were dead and buried.' But United – with such stars as Schmeichel, Irwin, Kanchelskis, Ince and Giggs – were to win their one and only League Cup, with a single Brian McClair goal.

But it had been an excellent season for Keane personally, with the youngster scooping the Player of the Year Award at the City Ground, the Barclays Young Eagle of the Year Award and ending up as one of the most talked-about midfielders in the Premiership. In March 1992, he had renewed his contract to remain with Forest. But, most importantly, he had negotiated a get-out clause if the club were to drop a division.

Relegation became a reality the following season. Despite Keane's battling – 'He stood out head and shoulders above all others, hence Man U came in,' said one fan

– Forest went down. But there were many battling displays, and the fans were looking to Keane to save Nottingham Forest from the drop. They had optimism, as displayed in December 1992, when Nigel Clough and Roy Keane destroyed Spurs' eight-match unbeaten run. Clough pulled the defence all over the pitch, setting up a first goal for Ian Woan, and did the same for an impressive Keane to win the match. At the start of 1993 Roy was still committed to Forest. 'All I want to do at the moment is concentrate on playing football, although I've been involved in a lot of talks about a new contract. I'm very happy with the way they've gone and I honestly can't see any problem in signing when the season is over.' He made these comments after a match against fellow strugglers Oldham Athletic on 30 January, in which Roy was pushed into a forward position and helped lay on the goals for Ian Woan in a 2-0 win, which lifted the club off the bottom of the table for the first time in 22 weeks.

Frank Clark, who replaced Clough as manager at the end of the season, wanted to keep his star player, but the ambitious Keane didn't relish a spell down a division. By May 1993, Keane had agreed terms with Kenny Dalglish at Blackburn Rovers which would make him a millionaire at 21. The youngster underlined his usefulness on the pitch at the time by scoring after just 14 seconds in the David O'Leary testimonial against Hungary at Lansdowne Road. The Lancashire side had millions in the bank and was bankrolled by local multimillionaire Jack Walker, who had sold his company GKN to British Steel for £330 million. Dalglish offered Keane a massive pay rise from his £6,000 a week at Forest in a four-year contract offering a wage reckoned at £8,000–£10,000 a week. 'I want to win a Premier League medal and Blackburn are well equipped to do so,' said Keane, and the headline writers were delighted with the 'Roy of the Rovers' move.

By the end of May, Alex Ferguson – manager of league champions Manchester United – had joined the race for the star, saying, 'Roy is one of the best young midfielders in the game.' As late as 14 June, Roy commented: 'I'll be glad when the deal [with Blackburn] is done and everything is out in the open.' But a game of snooker at Alex Ferguson's home changed history. 'We didn't discuss contracts. We just talked about football,' Roy revealed. 'That's when I decided I was going to Manchester United. I was only talking to him for 60 seconds and I knew I was going to become a Manchester United player.'

Three days later, Manchester United chairman Martin Edwards told the media: 'I'm delighted to hear that Roy wants to sign for us and I'll be contacting Forest tomorrow.' But the sticking point was money, with Forest holding out for £5 million and United refusing to go over £3.5 million. In addition, Roy could expect nothing like £10,000 a week at Old Trafford, with its tight wage limits, and ambitious Arsenal had tabled a bid for £4 million. 'Blackburn have offered me a fabulous deal but money isn't everything,' said Keane, who would get £6,000 a week at United. 'I've always wanted to play for Manchester United and the prospect of European Cup football makes me even more determined to go there.' And the former Spurs fan added: 'All my family follow them [United], and I just couldn't actually say no to Manchester United.'

By 16 July, Forest had agreed to a United bid of £3.75 million, the highest ever for an Irish player. Cobh Ramblers had lost out on a payout of up to £700,000 because of the lack of a sell-on clause in their deal three years before. But United were ecstatic. 'This deal took place because of Roy Keane's attitude. He never once came back to us and asked United to match what Blackburn were offering,' said Martin Edwards. 'The deal is as good as done,' said Forest's assistant manager, Alan Hill. 'We are quite happy with their bid. Roy will become a United player this weekend.'

Manchester United had already booked Keane a place on the plane to their pre-season trip to South Africa . . .

4

'I Thought He Was A Great Buy For United.'

Manchester United's former Captain Marvel, Bryan Robson, could be forgiven for harbouring ill feelings towards Roy Keane. The Corkman really came to Alex Ferguson's attention during a tense match at Old Trafford between the Red Devils and Nottingham Forest in the '91–'92 season. Keane unceremoniously careered into Robson in front of the United faithful of the Stretford End. 'The bloody cheek of him,' Ferguson admits to thinking at the time, but the manager clearly grew to respect that confident swagger on the field. When Roy did sign for Manchester United, it looked as if Robson was on the way out of the club he had served so well since his signing by Ron Atkinson in 1981. In the '93–'94 season, he was handed the No 12 jersey as Roy Keane took Robson's usual midfield place in the Charity Shield against Arsenal, and the 36-year-old veteran – capped 90 times for England – was consigned to the bench.

In the circumstances, it would be understandable if the Middlesbrough manager – who played 326 times for United, scoring 74 goals – were to regret the day he saw Keane, but this would be wide of the mark. In fact, Robson says he gave his seal of approval when the club was toying with the idea of signing the young Irishman.

'I remember I was sitting having a cup of tea in the coach's room – after years at Old Trafford I was allowed to do that! – and they were chatting about Roy. Alex Ferguson was saying would they pay £3.5 million or so to Forest; I remember them talking about that. Alex asked me and I gave the thumbs up.'

Perhaps it was because of Roy's nature, which reminded Robson of himself skills-wise – 'I think we are similar in that we had this bit of all-round ability' – and his never-say-die attitude. Bryan could also be forgiven for wincing at the memory of his games against the young Forest upstart. 'I remember playing against Roy a couple of times – it was always a tough battle with Forest, and they were a useful side. Roy was a good young player, and with him you always knew you were in a game.'

But he enjoyed it better with Roy playing alongside him, not against him. 'He is an excellent player – for me, one of the best in the game, all-round. He has a bit of everything – he's a good passer, he's quick, he's great in the air and he's a strong tackler.' And Roy acknowledges that the old master showed him how to improve as a player and become a box-to-box battler in his mould. 'He's a fit lad; that's why his stamina is good and his strength is good.' Robson reveals that even a sore head couldn't stop Roy from standing out at the Cliff during match preparations. 'He's a great trainer, even after he was out for a few drinks the night before! He was not one to stand in the wings.'

Robson – winner of the European Cup Winners' Cup in

1991 – cheered United along as they chased the European Cup in Barcelona. And, on the night, his thoughts turned to the suspended Paul Scholes and Roy Keane. 'It must have been really disappointing for him, but he handled it great in front of the media. Deep down it must have really hurt.' And he was as shocked as other Man United fans when Roy got a yellow card for a late tackle on Juventus's Zinedine Zidane in April. A yellow that put him out of the final. 'It was a nothing thing, that challenge in the semi-final. To miss the greatest night for United must have been really disappointing. But I think he will have another chance; there's a chance this team will be together for years. And no, I can't see Roy leaving United now, whatever the interest from Italy.'

But he would be tempted to take the battler on his books at Middlesbrough: 'I definitely wouldn't mind Roy in my team – we'd be a stronger team with him!'

5

'We're Playing Other Sides Off The Park.'

The Theatre of Dreams at Old Trafford: joining up with world superstars such as Peter Schmeichel, Eric Cantona and Ryan Giggs. As Roy put it: 'If you can't turn it on in a stadium like this, with all those fans urging you on, you'll never do it.' Roy's only worry was that his combative style at Forest might have made him some enemies at his new club, and he admitted having had run-ins in the past with Schmeichel, Paul Ince, Gary Pallister, Steve Bruce and Lee Sharpe. But the pre-season trip to South Africa, taking in some of its most poverty-stricken shanty towns, cemented his relationship with his new team-mates, and he was in the starting line-up for the FA Charity Shield match against Arsenal, which United won 5-4 on penalties.

In the weeks and months to come, Roy would become a firm favourite with the fans – even if they were already spoiled by the skills of the best team in the land – but the early days were a baptism of fire. Top division football with an above-average team like Forest was one thing; treading the turf of the Busby Babes, Denis Law, George Best and Norman Whiteside was an entirely different affair. 'I've been taken aback by the fanaticism of the fans,' he revealed. 'I went into the office to collect my pay slip and I nearly never got out of the place.' And he added that the champions' regime was not an easy one. 'The attention to detail here is unbelievable. At Forest, you could stroll in an hour before a match. Here, you must show up three hours early and have a meal of pasta.' And the superfit sportsman revealed a passion for junk food! 'I was always a great cheeseburger man but the dietician says it's a minus to eat too many of them.'

The new diet, combined with top-class coaching at the club's Cliff training ground, improved Roy by leaps and bounds. And it wasn't long before the Red faithful were roaring a now-familiar tune of 'Keano, Keano' at Old Trafford. He blasted two goals past Republic of Ireland keeper Alan Kelly on his home debut against Sheffield United on 18 August 1993. Tellingly, he vowed: 'The best is yet to come,' adding: 'I would have loved to have completed the hat-trick, but, as the song goes, "two out of three ain't bad".' Manager Alex Ferguson was delighted with the Corkman's gritty performance. 'Those two goals will have paid back £100 off his massive fee already,' he joked. And he paid Roy a huge compliment, comparing him with team-mate and United legend Bryan Robson. 'Roy is still so young that I know he is going to develop into an even better player than he is,' he added. 'He makes those runs that Robbo used to make, and by arriving at the right time he's always going to score goals for us.' Keane himself wasn't too fazed by the pressure. 'The worst part of the day for me was waiting for the game. I was just lying around in my hotel bedroom waiting for the time to go.'

With his first Premiership trophy in the bag from the '92-'93 season, Alex Ferguson looked towards the European Cup – now called the Champions League – which was seen as the Scotsman's 'holy grail'. English clubs had fallen behind their continental counterparts in terms of skill and tactics since the last team – Liverpool in 1985 – had appeared in a European Cup final. The season before, United had tumbled embarrassingly out of the UEFA Cup to Torpedo Moscow, having lost 4-3 on penalties. David Beckham, Gary Neville and Nicky Butt were among the subs at the home leg to the Russian giants.

Man-of-the-moment Keane was viewed by Ferguson as the key to an assault on Europe. He described him as 'a huge plus' for the squad as they prepared to take on Hungarian champs Kispest-Honved on 15 September. Keane – the subject of interest from continental clubs when he was quitting Forest – launched himself on the European stage with a blistering display against hapless Honved. He scored two goals away in Budapest, in the eighth and forty-second minute, with Eric Cantona claiming the other United goal. The Reds won 3-2 – a dream result in their first European Cup tie since 15 May 1969.

But Keane was eager to play down the hype surrounding his European debut, stating that he was glad to be playing at all after a poor display in a previous match out on the right wing rather than a preferred centre-of-midfield position. 'I played there at Chelsea on Saturday and I was crap,' he admitted. 'I was lucky the boss kept me in his starting 11 after that performance. I like to get up and down the middle but I hate it when I have time on the ball. That's the weakest part of my game.' And Fergie revealed, 'He always threatens when he gets in behind people and he did that all night. That's his strong point.'

Keane was fast becoming a hero among the Old Trafford masses, and legends queued up to praise the Irishman's recent performances. 'At United, you are expected to do something extraordinary – Roy fits the bill perfectly in scoring the goals that he does,' said former goal-scoring great Bobby Charlton. The original king of the Stretford End, Denis Law, also paid tribute to the tough-tackler: 'Roy is going to have to be brave to carry on with the job. He will carry nasty bruises and maybe have a few broken bones from time to time. But I doubt if it will bother him.' Sponsors were also taking an interest in the midfield dynamo, and Roy signed a boot deal with Hi-Tec for £110,000 – the first commercial agreement organised for a player by the Professional Footballers Association.

The team was tipped to retain the Premier League title after seeing out August at the top of the table, with four wins, plus one draw, against emerging force Newcastle United. A Gavin Peacock goal in Keane's 'crap' match resulted in a 1-0 win for the West Londoners, United's first setback of the long campaign.

Worse was to come in Europe. The trip away to Turkish

giants Galatasary provided one of the lower points of the Red Devils' history. 'Welcome to the hell,' the banners eerily proclaimed in the teeming city of Istanbul. United, having surrendered a two-goal lead only to trail 3–2 at home, were spared their blushes by a last-gasp Cantona effort. A more organised display was vital, but the football took a back seat in the cauldron of Alisamiyen Stadium on 3 November. 'The nightmare of the first leg haunted us right through the second match,' Ferguson admitted. The local authorities intimidated fans, Roy Keane was accused of spitting at Galatasaray striker Kubilay and Eric Cantona was allegedly attacked by a police officer after being red-carded for complaining about Turkish time-wasting. Manchester United went out, with a bitter taste in their mouths, in a 3–3 draw on the away-goals rule.

United could expect no sympathy from archrivals Manchester City at Maine Road the following Sunday – and it looked from the off as if the Reds were suffering a Euro hangover. The televised match showed the away side in disarray as City went into a 2-0 lead by half-time. But the mentally tough champions were not prepared to suffer more shame. Eric Cantona scored twice to level the game, with victory now up for grabs as City fell apart. With three minutes to spare, Roy Keane slid in to score the winner, sending the visiting fans delirious. Manchester United now looked set to retain their Championship title – at least according to the media pundits. In the 21 games up to Christmas, United won 16, drew 4 and lost just 1, with Roy featuring in 18 ties and scoring two goals against Sheffield United, one against Spurs, and one against City.

But United were being chased all the way by the team Roy had snubbed, big-spending Blackburn Rovers. The two giants clashed on St Stephen's Day, with the visitors going a goal up at Old Trafford and fiercely resisting any equaliser. With two minutes to go, Paul Ince achieved the point for United, who were to draw 0-0 at home to Leeds United on New Year's Day. The next match, at Anfield, shook United's title hopes as the away team, 3-0 up with goals from Steve Bruce, Ryan Giggs and Denis Irwin, delivered only a 3-3 draw.

The club was in mourning on 20 January, when news came through of the death of Sir Matt Busby, the architect of all of United's post-war glory. The championship pennant flew at half-mast as Keane and the other players contested the next match, at home to Everton. Three days after Sir Matt's funeral, his winning legacy continued as United defeated Norwich City in the fourth round of the FA Cup. After Keano and Cantona scored in the 2-0 win, fans were asking themselves if the club could even achieve more than the previous year and win both the league and the FA Cup. Even an unprecedented treble was a possibility after the defeat of Sheffield Wednesday in the first leg of the Coca-Cola Cup semi-final.

But those hopes were dashed after a rash of crippling suspensions. Goalkeeper Peter Schmeichel was to miss the Coca-Cola Cup final, Eric Cantona got two red cards in three days and winger Andrei Kanchselskis was sent off in the Wembley final, which Aston Villa won 3-1. Eric Cantona's first red card during that period – for stamping on John Moncur's chest – overshadowed Roy Keane's goal in that 2-2 draw against lowly Swindon Town. Three days later, the Frenchman was hard done by after getting the red after his second bookable offence at Highbury against Arsenal.

But Keane's first season at Old Trafford was a glorious one, with Manchester United completing their first-ever double of league and FA Cup wins. On 1 May, United won away to Ipswich Town at Portman Road, while title-chasers Blackburn Rovers slumped to defeat at Coventry City, giving United their first back-to-back title victories since the days of the Busby Babes in the 1956-'57 season. It was veteran midfielder Bryan Robson's last league game for his club, and he was stunned to be left out of the line-up for the FA Cup final against Chelsea, with Keane partnering Paul Ince in midfield. Two penalties from Cantona and one goal each from Mark Hughes and Brian McClair gave Keano his first taste of FA Cup victory.

Roy had found glory, too, in the green jersey since his debut in 1992. In the first World Cup qualifier – at home to Latvia – on 9 September 1992, Ireland stormed to a 4-0 final as they aimed to emulate their Italia '90 success, when they made it to the quarter-finals only to be narrowly defeated by the host nation. In the next game, away to Denmark, Roy was aiming to score against future team-mate Peter Schmeichel. Ireland returned home after a creditable 0-0 draw against the reigning European champions. Away to Spain in Seville in December '92, Keane shone in a goalless draw that Ireland should have won after a legitimate John Aldridge goal was deemed to be offside. After the game, Maradonna described Keano as one of the best young midfielders in Europe, stating, 'He is one of the few players to have impressed me this year.' Despite wins against Northern Ireland, Albania, Latvia (away) and Lithuania (home and away), Keane and co were hammered 3-1 at home by the Spanish.

The Republic were left needing at least a point against old rivals Northern Ireland on the tense turf of Windsor Park in Belfast. Before the game, Republic fans were warned not to travel, and many questioned the logic of playing a crunch tie in such a hostile atmosphere. Jimmy Quinn gave Northern Ireland the lead, and the Republic looked doomed to lose out to Denmark in the battle for a World Cup place. But substitute Alan McLoughlin, partnering Keane, scored the vital goal – Ireland were through to the finals. Unforgettably, Keane turned the air blue with expletives as he roared his excitement and hugged McLoughlin and his other team-mates.

Keane played some of his finest games for Ireland in America, stifling the Italians as Ireland achieved a memorable victory in Giants Stadium. He battled through 110-degree heat as Ireland lost to Mexico in Orlando and single-handedly bossed Norway around back in New

York. Although a 2-0 loss to Holland ended Ireland's World Cup campaign, Roy Keane had made his mark on world football.

6

The 1994-'95 Season

United had achieved the double; Roy Keane had been Ireland's player of USA '94 – how could things get better for the Corkman? The fact is, they didn't. After the highs of the previous season, Manchester United – on course for a double – lost the league to Blackburn Rovers and the FA Cup to Everton. The season, though, will forever be remembered for one thing – the Cantona kung-fu kick. Away games to Crystal Palace are never easy affairs for United, with the local fans always desperate to embarrass the visiting giants. The night of 25 January 1995 was no exception. After Eric Cantona, the victim of late tackles and violent challenges, was sent off after losing his cool and fouling Palace defender Richard Shaw, a local Palace fan ran to the bottom of the Selhurst Park stand to pour scorn on the Frenchman. He later claimed that he had roared, 'It's an early shower for you, mate.' Others remember a rather more abusive comment, and Cantona lunged across a McDonald's advertising sign not once, but twice, hitting the supporter in the midriff with a kung-fu-style kick. 'The Twit Hits the Fan', the tabloids roared the following day, and United's title dreams were also to get the boot.

Even at the start of the season, the United fans were hoping for big-name signings and were disappointed to lure just one player – former Blackburn defender David May – to Old Trafford, for £1.2 million. By 10 December, when a Keane goal helped his team beat QPR 3-2, United were just one point behind Kenny Dalglish's Blackburn Rovers. The Mancunians had lost just three times – 2-1 away to Leeds, 3-2 away to Ipswich Town, and 1-0 away to Sheffield Wednesday. And mounting injuries, although not taking a toll, were worrying, given Blackburn's impressive league form. Roy Keane, Peter Schmeichel, Ryan Giggs and Lee Sharpe all needed treatment by mid-season.

But United had been humiliated in Europe, and despite impressive wins at first they were out of the Champions League before Christmas. A Keane-less United had convincingly despatched Sweden's Gothenburg in the first tie, at Old Trafford, on 14 September, winning 4-2 with goals from Lee Sharpe, Andrei Kanchelskis and Ryan Giggs, who scored twice. The previous year's hated rivals, Galatasaray, held United to a goalless draw in Istanbul, and Manchester next faced European giants Barcelona at home. The English champions were facing such greats as Ronald Koeman in defence, Miguel 'The Beast' Nadal and Gheroghe Hagi in defence and Hristo Stoichkov in attack.

At home, Peter Schmeichel, Paul Parker, Denis Irwin, David May, Nicky Butt, Gary Pallister, Andrei Kanchelskis, Paul Ince, Roy Keane, Mark Hughes and Lee Sharpe took the game to the visitors, and the thrilling encounter ended in a 2-2 draw, on 19 October. The away leg a fortnight later was a different matter. The foreigners rule – limiting the number of non-English players Man United could field – seriously depleted the team at the Nou Camp. Gary Walsh replaced Peter Schmeichel in goal, and he and Eric Cantona sat together in the stands as their team was slaughtered by the Catalan giants. Brazilian forward Romario and Stoichkov tore United apart, and Keane, Ince and other United heroes were given a masterclass in football. Despite a goal from Roy Keane in the 4-0 revenge mission against Galatasaray five days after the Nou Camp drubbing, United had already lost to Gothenburg away 3-1, so they went out at the group stage of the competition.

Manchester City were unfortunate to be the next team to face their local rivals, and the Reds went on a wrecking spree, beating City 5-0 at a match televised to millions by Sky Television. Kanchelskis got a hat-trick, with the other goals coming from Mark Hughes and Eric Cantona. Ten days into the New Year, Andy Cole was signed from Newcastle United in a £7 million deal that saw winger Keith Gillespie heading in the opposite direction. Despite some marvellous league results – a 9-0 drubbing of Ipswich Town, in which Roy scored; a 1-0 victory over title-race leaders Blackburn; and a 3-0 victory over Arsenal – Blackburn Rovers, the most expensive team in English history, won the league by a single point.

In the FA Cup, Keane was involved in perhaps the most controversial red-card incident of his year after he stamped on Crystal Palace defender Gareth Southgate in the FA Cup semi-final at Villa Park and Palace man Darren Patterson was sent off for attacking the Irishman in a flare-up on the pitch. The incident occurred in a stormy match that the FA didn't appreciate, as it followed the death of a Palace fan in an altercation with United supporters. Keane was fined a week's wages by the club, served a three-match ban and was fined £5,000 by the FA for a disrepute charge. In Keane's defence his reaction occurred after a clumsy challenge by Southgate. An X-ray later revealed ligament damage and a chipped ankle bone. Earlier, Roy Keane had to have seven stitches to the same ankle. Alex Ferguson admitted: 'It's a bad blow for us. We knew it was a bad tackle but the extent of the damage was not readily apparent.'

Keane did make it to Wembley – but he might have wished he hadn't bothered. A 1-0 loss to Everton thanks to a Paul Rideout goal in the lacklustre FA Cup final capped a depressing year, in which the double-chasers had won nothing, bar the Charity Shield.

7

The 1995-'96 Season

Although 1995 saw the return of the Magnificent 7 and chants of 'Ooh-ahh, Cantona' around Old Trafford – yes, Monsieur Cantona was set to return to Old Trafford, after his ban – the year had begun with fans calling for Ferguson's head. Andrei Kanchelskis was out the door, leaving for Everton; goal-scoring hero Mark Hughes had been sold to Chelsea; Paul Ince's midfield services were no longer required and he was on the way to Inter Milan. In came unfamiliar faces – David Beckham, the Neville brothers, Paul Scholes and Nicky Butt. When Roy Keane and the youngsters slumped to a first-day 3-1 defeat to Aston Villa, the knives were being sharpened for Ferguson. On Match of the Day, Alan Hansen summed up the prevailing mood by saying that you won't win anything with kids. He was never to live that remark down.

With the team attempting to get into its stride, Roy Keane was at his battling best, scoring a goal in the 2-1 victory over West Ham in the next game. After he passed the ball into the Hammers' net at Old Trafford, he was engulfed by the rising young stars. In the following game, against Wimbledon, he scored twice as the Dons were destroyed 3-1. His first goal was a neat one-two with Paul Scholes, while his second was a goal-poacher's delight: he nipped in after the keeper failed to hold a Lee Sharpe blast. Both times, Roy raised his fists to the fans in triumph.

But two days later, controversy followed the Corkman on to the pitch yet again. Away to Blackburn Rovers at Ewood Park, he was running on to goal in an action-packed match. Only Scottish defender Colin Hendry stood in his path. The imposing centre-half tripped Keane by accident as he lunged for the ball, and Roy went sprawling in the penalty area. Keane was sent off for his second bookable offence because the ref believed he had dived. TV playbacks showed that Keane had received the harshest card decision of his career. Worse was to come: at a bad-tempered game against Bryan Robson's Middlesbrough, Keane was sent off. He served his suspension while recovering from his second hernia operation of the season.

At first, the team seemed able to cope without the presence of Keane and other first-teamers, winning comfortably against Southampton and Coventry City. But during December, the team struggled, drawing with Chelsea and Sheffield Wednesday and losing to Liverpool.

The two crunch ties of the year were against new title threats Newcastle United. At home in a tension-packed Theatre of Dreams on an icy 27 December, United faced skilful French winger David Ginola, free-scoring centre-forward Les Ferdinand and accomplished midfielder Rob Lee. A first goal, from Andy Cole, took Cole's old club by surprise, while at the other end great goalkeeping by Schmeichel kept out Ferdinand. With Keane waving his hands in the air and timing his run into the box with perfection, he was found by David Beckham. Roy controlled the ball just outside the six-yard box and buried a shot in the bottom right-hand corner, past the oncoming keeper Pavel Srinicek.

In the away fixture at St James's Park, with the match being broadcast to millions by Sky, Keane snuffed out Newcastle's runs and the visitors went home 1-0 winners after an exhausting encounter. 'It took us about a week to recover,' Keane later revealed.

Newcastle United – originally 12 points clear at the top of the table – were left level with them on points but behind on goal difference by mid-March. The astonishing work-rate of Eric Cantona had powered United up the table, and Keane was dominating teams in midfield, with even the likes of player-manager Ruud Gullit's Chelsea finding it difficult to gain possession, let alone goals, in a 4-1 drubbing at home at Stamford Bridge. Keane's work-rate and skill hadn't gone unnoticed on the continent either.

But Man United came unstuck by April. After a 1-0 victory against Coventry City on April 8, Manchester were six points clear at the top of the table, with a goal difference of 31 to Newcastle's 26. But the next match – away to Southampton – saw one of the most embarrassing defeats in the club's history. Beckham, Giggs and Butt badly underperformed at the Dell. Ferguson blamed the team's grey strip, complaining that the players could not see one another. At half-time, 3-0 down, the visitors changed to blue-and-white-striped shirts and pulled a goal back at the death.

Newcastle won their next game, with United up against fierce rivals Leeds United at home on 17 April. The omens looked good for United after Leeds keeper Mark Beeney was sent off in the thirteenth minute for handling the ball outside the area. Defender Lucas Radebe came off the bench and thwarted every United effort on goal. Season hero Eric Cantona was strangely off-form against his old club, and the Red Army could see another league title slipping out of the team's grasp.

With no ideas on how to break down the ten-man defensive wall put up by Leeds, United heads went down. Yet again, leadership was needed – and it was provided by Roy Keane. He struck a blistering shot from outside the box which blasted into the net at the old Stretford End. It had taken 73 minutes to get the vital goal which kept Manchester United in the championship driving seat. As the *Daily Mail* correspondent put it: 'The word "prolific" could not be attached to Roy Keane's prowess as a goalscorer, but Old Trafford could not have cared a fig for that last night.'

After a 5-0 hammering of Keane's old club, Nottingham Forest, and a 3-0 away win to Bryan Robson's Middlesbrough, United were champions yet again. Now for the double double.

No English team had ever achieved two doubles; most

AIRBORNE: Roy in flight during the 1997 World Cup Qualifier away in Skopje.
© INPHO

ALL AMERICAN HERO: Roy and Phil Babb were true heroes for Ireland in the World Cup in New York and Orlando.
© Independent Newspapers

FIT FOR A KING: The star's new mock Tudor home in upmarket Hale Barns in Cheshire.
© Independent Newspapers

SIX OF THE BEST: Holding off Sainovski Dzevdet of Macedonia in the World Cup Qualifier 1997 away in Skopje.
© INPHO

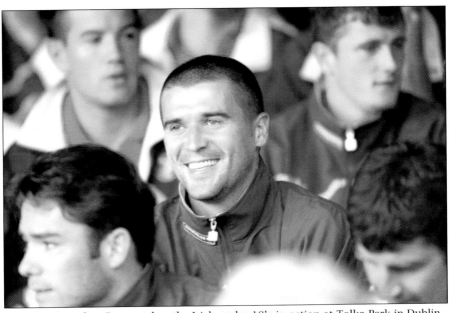

TIME OUT: A smiling Roy watches the Irish under-18's in action at Tolka Park in Dublin.
© Independent Newspapers

GOAL-DEN WONDER: Celebrating a goal against Malta in October 1998 in the European qualifier at Lansdowne Road.
© INPHO

Taking it on the Chin: Roy Keane extends a greeting to a Lithuanian player in Dublin in August 1998.
© INPHO

De Boer War: The ecstasy of the victory over Italy at USA '94 turned to the agony of a 2-0 defeat by Holland in Orlando. Here, Roy takes on world star Frank de Boer.
© INPHO

SHALL WE DANCE: Roy in training for Ireland with Tony Cascarino and Jeff Kenna.
© Independent Newspapers

FANCY FOOTWORK: The player has risen from putting the gear out at Forest to signing lucrative boot deals with Diadora.
© Independent Newspapers

HEADS HE WINS: Managers such as Alex Ferguson and Brian Clough have regarded Roy as twice the player of anybody else in the English League.
©INPHO

IT'S ALL A YAWN: Despite impressive performances, Roy's commitment to the Republic has been questioned by critics.
© INPHO

JOLLY GREEN GIANT: Roy has a laugh in training for Ireland in Clonshaugh, Co. Dublin in 1998.
© INPHO

LEADERS OF MEN: At Clonshaugh with Ireland boss, Mick McCarthy.
© INPHO

LEADING BY EXAMPLE: Captain Fantastic troops his men into battle.
© INPHO

GAME OF TWO HALVES: Roy, pictured leaving the pitch after the away defeat to Yugoslavia in Belgrade in 1998, has experienced glory and notoriety playing for Ireland.
© INPHO

MASSIVE DEAL: In Dublin to promote Diadora boots as part of his contract with the sports giants.
© Independent Newspapers

OUTSTANDING IN HIS FIELD: Keane has graced the likes of Wembley, the San Siro and Giants Stadium.
© Independent Newspapers

LINING OUT: The likes of Gary Kelly, Ian Harte, Roy and Kenny Cunningham take on Iceland in Reykjavik in 1997.
© INPHO

MEXICAN WAVE: In the heat of the action in Orlando against Mexico in June '94.
© Sportsfile

WORLD BEATERS: Lining up with such heroes as David O'Leary, now manager of Leeds United, Ray Houghton and Andy Townsend.
© Sportsfile

UNITED IRELAND: Old Trafford's Cork-born heroes Denis Irwin and Roy.
© Sportsfile

PROUD LEADER: Composed before another outing with Ireland.
© Sportsfile

THE HEAT IS ON: The Irish team struggled against soaring temperatures in Orlando in the tie against Mexico during USA '94.
© INPHO

would have happily settled for one. Roy Keane was at his imperious best in midfield against Liverpool at Wembley in the FA Cup final. In a dull match, a goal seemed unlikely. But in the eighty-fifth minute, Liverpool keeper David James punched the ball clear from a corner. It bounced off Ian Rush's shoulder, only to land in the path of Eric Cantona, who blasted the ball through a crowded box. Keane was the first to hug the Gallic genius, and Keane, not Cantona, was the Man of the Match. As the captain showboated to the crowd – and gave away possession – Keane roared abuse at him and strangled any forward runs by the Merseysiders. United were victorious, double-double winners, but history will probably forget Keane's vital contribution at Wembley, even though he had been voted Man of the Match by the BBC.

And Alan Hansen wisely admitted that he had made a gaffe in his comments about kids . . .

8

The 1996-'97 Season

'I actually live quite a boring life'

Keane uttered those immortal words in an interview published in the *Irish Independent*. He was referring to his private life and the tales of excess that have dogged him since his move into the spotlight at Britain's biggest club. According to Keane, he likes to do his talking on the pitch. After three years at the club, he began to grow in stature. Although he scored just two goals in the entire season, he was United's rock, its soul, encouraging the 'youngsters' in the team – mostly only a few years younger than himself – to greater heights. With the arrival of Czech winger Karel Poborsky, Barcelona veteran Jordi Cruyff, and Norwegians Ronnie Johnsen and Ole Gunnar Solskjaer, United aimed to win on all fronts and make a determined assault on the Champions League.

But even after the 4-0 humiliation of Newcastle United in the Charity Shield, in which he scored against Man United's big northeastern rivals, Keane faced a new worry, with another knee operation pencilled in. He was to make 33 appearances for Manchester United in '96-'97, five fewer than in the previous season.

In Europe, United performed well, beating Rapid Vienna 2-0 in both legs, and had hopes of getting out of the qualifying group, despite losing their proud unbeaten home record in Europe to Turkish unknowns Fenerbache. Roy got his first taste of action against the might of Juventus when the team lost 1-0 away to the Italians on 20 November. But Manchester United did make it through to the next round of the competition, where they faced a daunting task against the impressive FC Porto, who had disposed of AC Milan in their qualifying group. Up to an hour before the kick-off, Europe's media did not know if Roy Keane would be able to play the tie, after his recent injuries. The team-sheet showed no sign of the Corkman, but Manchester United overwhelmed Porto, destroying them 4-0 in one of their best-ever European performances. Defeats to Borussia Dortmund ended United's interest in the competition, but the team had shown it could score at will in Europe and would become a force to be reckoned with.

In the league, Roy Keane and his team-mates under-performed as Southampton beat them 6-3 at the Dell, but Keane could not be blamed for a previous humiliation – the 5-0 away defeat to Newcastle United – as he was absent from the team. The situation had improved by April '97, however, with Roy playing his part in the title chase. The 3-1 defeat of Liverpool on Merseyside left United needing just four points from four games to win the title. Three draws – against Leicester City, 'Bro and Newcastle – and a final-day win at home to West Ham were more than enough to retain the title, with a poor 75 points in a poor Premiership race.

Controversy dogged Keane at international level, too,

with Irish newspapers devoting thousands of column-inches to his absences from games. Mick McCarthy, who replaced Jack Charlton as Ireland manager after the team's failure to reach the Euro '96 finals, enjoyed Keane's presence for just one of his first ten games in charge. The club-level star had been absent through injury, suspension or failure to show. The low point came when Roy – who had been made captain for McCarthy's first game, a friendly against Russia – was sent off for a bad tackle in the dying seconds of the game. The former Millwall manager and Republic of Ireland defender also offered Keane the captaincy for the US tour in June 1996, but Keane, in 'mix-up', had gone away on holidays to Capri. In all, Roy played three of the Republic's 20 internationals up to 20 October 1996, missing key games against Portugal at Lansdowne Road and the 'Stadium of Light' the home clash with Austria and the Euro '96 play-off against Holland in Anfield.

But 20 October proved to be a turning point. In the World Cup qualifiers, McCarthy needed Roy's experience in an injury-depleted side to take on Iceland in Dublin. Stand-in centre-half Keane was insulted by small sections of the crowd, who were prompted by some pundits to boo the Corkman. But a few timely tackles, and seemingly effortless domination of midfield and the back, turned the crowd, and the player has rarely looked back since at international level, helping the team towards qualification for the European Championships in 2000.

9

THE 1997-'98 SEASON

'I actually heard the ligament tear as I went down.'

Yet another Premiership title in the bag; the Charity Shield won on 3 August against Chelsea; a lucrative boot deal. Just as everything was going so well, the cruel hand of fate was to touch Roy again. Eric Cantona had said au revoir to Old Trafford on 18 May, the day after Chelsea had beaten Middlesbrough in the FA Cup final. United depended on a new captain to inspire them at home and in Europe; battling Roy was the perfect candidate.

Although his playing was to suffer, his bank balance didn't, and Roy was snapped up by Diadora UK in a deal estimated to be worth £2 million to him.

'Myself and the managing director at the time, my brother Chris, had two reasons for signing Keano,' says Diadora UK boss Andrew Ronay, a keen Manchester United fan. 'Firstly, he was one of the most influential players in the Premiership, and secondly it gave great brand recognition in southern Ireland.' In the past, the company has signed the Neville brothers and Andy Townsend, but Keane was a coup, and controversial posters proclaiming, 'We've sold our soul to the devil' popped up in cities. But Roy's reputation is undeserved, Ronay believes. 'I can honestly say that he was great to deal with. He's just one of the lads and is someone you can relate to; some players you just can't relate to.'

And Ronay is glad the company showed commitment to Roy when his cruciate injury occurred: 'Every sports company has a clause that says if such a thing happens, it can review the deal. I openly said at the time we would not do it.' He adds that he 'was gutted' at the time of Keane's crisis.

But no one was more gutted than Roy himself. Aside from the Charity Shield, Roy was to play just ten games in total for the entire season and watch from the sidelines as Manchester United chased an unprecedented treble of league title, FA Cup and European Cup. In the end United would win sweet FA, and Alex Ferguson admitted that Roy's absence had been the reason for a trophy-less season at Old Trafford.

In a dream start to the season, Captain Keane had scored two goals – against Coventry City and West Ham – as his side remained undefeated at league and European level. Then came the match at Elland Road on 27 September. Not a place for the faint-hearted, the Leeds ground is a cauldron of tension for United players and fans alike, as many home fans vent their bile with their 'We only hate Man United' chants and mock the victims of the Munich air disaster.

In a rash challenge on Leeds midfielder Alf Inge Haaland, Keane fell awkwardly and hobbled off the pitch, to the taunts of the crowd. For once the headline writers were to be spot on in their predictions: 'No Cantona, no Keane – no chance'. But others were to rub salt into Roy's wounds. Many pundits felt he had deserved his fate, something which upsets him. 'I didn't try to break his leg or his neck,' he told one interviewer. 'I nearly lost my career and people say I deserve what happened.'

Ireland manager Mick McCarthy felt for his midfielder. 'No player wants any injury but this is the one everybody wants least of all,' he said. 'Right now my thoughts are with the player and his family. It is terrible news and all we can do is offer him our full support – if or when he needs it.' A spokesman at Old Trafford revealed the following week: 'He had an exploratory operation on Monday when a small piece of cartilage was removed and it was discovered that he would also require a cruciate knee ligament operation. That will be performed in approximately four weeks when the swelling goes down. He will be out for the rest of the season.' Alex Ferguson was shocked by the injury, but would not buy cover for the European campaign as the continent's top footballers would most likely be involved in cup matches and ineligible to play for United. 'It goes without saying that it is a bad blow for us and my thoughts on just how important a player he is to us have been well documented on many occasions. He has played a major part in our success and is an inspirational kind of player,' Ferguson said. But he revealed his optimism regarding Keane's long-term future: 'In the past it was viewed as a career-threatening type of thing but many players now successfully recover and I have absolutely no doubt that Roy Keane will be back for next season.'

Keane himself remembered: 'I knew as soon as it happened that the injury was very serious . . . I actually heard the ligament tear as I went down and I told our physio, Dave Fevre, it was bad. I was 90 per cent sure it was the cruciate before I had the first operation, so it wasn't a surprise when the specialist told me when I woke up. At least he told me out straight. He just said, "the knee is knackered," but I already knew.'

While Roy and United winger Terry Cooke prepared for similar operations, it was business as usual on the pitch for the rest of the team. Despite injuries to two keepers – Peter Schmeichel and stand-in Raimond van der Gouw – the team was 12 points clear at the top of the table after defeating Chelsea at Stamford Bridge on 28 February. In the FA Cup, United beat Chelsea 5-3 in the third round. At one stage in this match they were 5-0 up after two goals from Beckham – one a breathtaking free kick – two from new signing Teddy Sheringham and one from Andy Cole. In the next round, Walsall were dismissed 5-1 with goals from Cole, Solskjaer and Johnsen. In Europe, the mighty Juventus were outplayed and outfought at Old Trafford in a stunning 3-2 Manchester United win, made all the more memorable by an impressive dribbling run and goal from Ryan Giggs. United, top of the group, were through to the next round and looked unstoppable.

No one seemed to notice Keane's absence much; there were mutterings in the media about just how important he really was. Naturally, the injured player was going through agony in the stands. 'I'm not a good spectator when it comes to football,' he admitted, adding that it was 'a little strange' to watch the Juventus tie at home. Bill Shankly never talked to injured players, and United legend Denis Law reveals that he was ignored by his boss at Huddersfield Town, even when they were walking past one another in a corridor. Keane, though, just didn't want to be around performing players. 'I feel I'd almost be making a nuisance of myself,' he revealed at the time of his injury. But United's season began to fall apart as injuries halted them on all fronts. In the FA Cup, the team went out to Barnsley; in Europe they went out with a whimper to an above-average Monaco at Old Trafford. Pallister, Giggs, May, Keane, Scholes and Gary Neville were absent from the tie.

By 3 May, the Premiership race too was over, as the seemingly unstoppable Arsenal overtook a tired Manchester side. A single point separated the destined double-winners from the trophy-less losers.

10

The 1998-'99 Season

In interviews leading up to the season Roy Keane usually made a point of protesting his innocence, blaming his fouls and sendings-off on commitment, not malice. The protests normally fell on deaf ears. But the captain's armband, allied with the devastating cruciate injury, had made a difference. The fans wondered if the same Roy Keane would return from injury. In fact, a new improved version, without the on-pitch rows that had taken away the focus from his skills, returned to the Old Trafford pitch. Roy had changed; as a certain match on the night of 14 April proved. The FA Cup semi-final replay against Arsenal was a nail-biting, adrenalin-charged affair, even for those viewing from a barstool or an armchair. Keane had to sit out the final 15 minutes of normal time in the Villa Park players' bar after being sent off for his second yellow. Same old Keano? Not quite. Minutes later, up stepped Arsenal hotshot Dennis Bergkamp for a ninetieth-minute penalty, only for Schmeichel to push it away. Roy had to endure that – and half an hour more of extra time. But there were no tantrums, no sob stories, just a contentment that his sending-off hadn't let his team down. 'I've no arguments and the referee didn't have a choice because they were two mistimed tackles, and that's it,' he stated to the media afterwards. It was that kind of attitude that powered Manchester United towards an unprecedented treble.

Roy had played a mere ten games in the previous season. In this, the most successful in the club's history, he would make 52 starts, and would come off the subs' bench for two further games. It was clear how important he was to the cause: the 52 games put him joint second for the season with full-back Gary Neville, only two starts behind Peter Schmeichel. In Europe, he made the second-highest number of appearances and some of the most telling contributions.

United, who had chased the league in the previous season, ended up empty-handed. Now they were in the Champions League as Premiership runners-up, record defensive signing (£10.75 million) Jaap Stam was slated, despite an impressive showing in the World Cup, and even loyal fans questioned the £12.6 million spent on Aston Villa hitman Dwight Yorke. It looked as if it was going to be a season of misery after double-winners Arsenal outclassed the team 3-0 at Wembley in the Charity Shield in August, and David Beckham was booed by supporters keen to blame England's exit from the World Cup on his sending-off in the match against Argentina. And the opening day of the season proved no better, as average side Leicester City led United 2-1 at home even into the ninetieth minute. Only an injury-time free-kick spectacular from Beckham saved the points. This was an indication of the refusal to lose that would lead to such glory.

Villa were leading the title race – but United were still breathing down their necks and performing well at League, FA Cup and European level. By Christmas, the team had lost just three matches – to Arsenal and Sheffield Wednesday in the Premiership and to Spurs in the low-priority Worthington Cup. In that space of time, the team had faced the likes of Liverpool, Bayern Munich, Newcastle United, title leaders Villa, Spurs, Blackburn Rovers and Leeds United. Keane had scored against Leeds at home in a hard-fought 3-2 game – a feat that could only endear him even more to his loyal band of followers – and pulled off a cracking goal three games later in the crunch match against Bayern.

In a team effort across all competitions, Keane led by example, controlling the midfield; Beckham whipped in the pinpoint crosses to crack open defences; Ryan Giggs was back to his surging best and Jaap Stam was growing in stature with every game. Former manager Eddie O'Rourke is only one of those who have been involved with Roy who believes the handing of the captain's armband to him in 1997 was 'a masterstroke'.

'With all the youngsters around he has become sort of a daddy to them all, and no one dare mess with them.' Nowhere was this more apparent than in the away clash with Tottenham Hotspur on 12 December. White Hart Lane was a torrid place to be for young Beckham, who was barracked constantly by the local fans. The travelling Manchester United fans responded with roars of 'Argentina, Argentina' as the players got stuck in on the turf. After going two goals up through Ole Gunnar Solskjaer, United were to suffer a massive blow: the sending off of right-back Gary Neville. The decision turned the game, and Spurs drew with two devastating headers from defender Sol Campbell. Although Beckham is tougher than his image suggests, he was getting booted around the park, and statistics for all games reveal he is the most-fouled Red. After one late tackle from Spurs' Andy Sinton, Keane grabbed the Tottenham man by the collar and warned him not to repeat the mistake. In a bad-tempered, physical match, Keane managed to control his emotions after the Sinton incident and left it at that. Manager Alex Ferguson was not so calm after dropping two points, refusing to discuss the 'defeat' with the media after the match.

But he had little to moan about for the rest of the season. The loss of Brian Kidd, who moved on from working as Ferguson's assistant to manage Blackburn Rovers, was a massive blow, as was the 3-2 home defeat to 'Bro. But that humiliating loss was to prove a turning point. The United defence had conceded a total of 23 goals; losses that would have proved crippling had it not been for the team's free-scoring forwards Yorke, Cole and Solskjaer. After the 'Bro blushes, the team would not be beaten again – at any level!

Of the next 33 games, including the Barcelona final, United would win 23. Highlights included the demolition of Roy's old club Forest, 8-1, in which sub Ole Gunnar Solskjaer scored a record-breaking four goals in 20 minutes after coming off the subs' bench in the second half. And cries of 'Ole, Ole' reverberated around the Theatre of Dreams after the young Norwegian scored the winning goal in the fourth round of the FA Cup. Arch-rivals Liverpool had been competently defending a single-goal advantage through Michael Owen. But in the dying minutes, Dwight Yorke equalised and a replay at Anfield seemed inevitable. But Solskjaer cracked in a shot in a packed penalty box, and Keane, Irwin, Butt and co ecstatically lapped up a roar fit for heroes.

Of so many special days and nights around England, the one that will last longest in the memory was the clash against Arsenal in the FA Cup semi-final replay. A perfectly fine goal from Roy Keane was ruled offside in the dour first semi-final, and it ended goalless. But few United fans now regret the assistant referee's decision, as it set up one of the classic FA Cup ties of all time. Keane and Butt in the centre of the Villa Park pitch gave Emmanuel Petit and Patrick Vieira a torrid time and started the match with all guns blazing. Good work in the midfield set up David Beckham for a goal-of-the-month-style 20-yard curler after just 17 minutes, but Dennis Bergkamp equalised in the sixty-ninth minute through a deflected effort. Six minutes later, United hearts dropped when the master of midfield, Roy Keane, was sent off. Five minutes later, the game looked to be over as Nicolas Anelka rounded Schmeichel to put the ball in the back of the net. It was offside, and the agony and the ecstasy continued for both sets of fans. In the ninetieth minute, Phil Neville conceded a penalty, and the Reds looked set to lose their third game of the season to their North London rivals. Bergkamp's curler lacked power, and Schmeichel palmed it away to break the Dutchman's heart.

'I thought the same as everybody else,' Roy Keane admitted. 'You think you're out of the Cup when something like that happens.'

In a game full of incident, the greatest moment had yet to come. Eighteen minutes into extra time, and with just ten men, only a miracle could save United, who would be lucky even to make it to penalties as Arsenal got a grip on the game. But a sloppy ball from Vieira changed football history. The ball was intercepted by Ryan Giggs, who raced from ten yards inside his own half towards goal. At the edge of the penalty area, the Gunners' top-class defenders Martin Keown and Lee Dixon were left trailing and flailing as the Welsh wizard moved closer to goal, flicking the ball from left to right in a mazy run. As captain Tony Adams slid in in a bid to save his side, Giggs let fly with an unstoppable shot past David Seaman into the roof of the net. United were through to Wembley in the most thrilling game of a roller-coaster season. Keane coolly pondered the occasion. 'I watched the rest of the game in the bar. It's funny because I watched the last semi in the bar here too when I was sent off against Palace [in 1995]. It's getting to be a bit of a habit.'

But the Red Devils just couldn't stop scoring goals as

they tackled the mighty. In an action-packed March, for instance, they took on Internazionale twice, Chelsea twice, and Newcastle United and Everton, scoring ten goals and conceding just three. The following month was no easier, with the team facing mighty Juventus twice, Arsenal twice, Leeds United, Wimbledon and Sheffield Wednesday. They managed to score 11, let in 6 and lose no games!

After a typically tough encounter with Wimbledon, Roy Keane was back in the news. This time, the growing appreciation of him as a player was reflected by an adversary, Wimbledon skipper Robbie Earle. 'He is the best midfielder in the country, by far,' he stated. 'He is the most influential player at United now, without a doubt. He sits and holds and dictates their play. Keano is better than Patrick Vieira, because you cannot wind him up. Maybe a few years ago, yes. Not any more, though.'

Revealing that he thought Keane had 'matured, he holds his temper,' he could have embarrassed the hardman with the revelation: 'He caught me late today, down by the sideline – and then said sorry. I was a bit surprised about that, I have to tell you! A couple of years ago, I'd have jumped in at him, he'd have jumped back in my face, and we'd have been pulling each other apart.'

The only sad aspect was that his fellow professionals, and sportswriters, did not see things in the same way. Rumours of the United vote being split between Keane, Yorke and Beckham, meant both Footballer of the Year Awards went to an entirely different player: David

Ginola. But sportswriter Peter Fitton, writing in The *Sun*, best summed up the feelings of the United faithful about Keane: 'David Ginola, twice Footballer of the Year, should seek permission to walk in his shadow.'

As late as 16 May, the last day of the Premiership race, United could still have ended up with nothing. Arsenal, just one point behind them, needed to beat Villa away to have a chance of retaining their trophy. United needed to win at home against Spurs to ensure victory. Some of the visitors may have preferred to see the Reds of Manchester win rather than their North London neighbours, but the Spurs team played to win, with Les Ferdinand opening the scoring. In a man-of-the-match performance, Keane battled in midfield, aiming to prevent a repeat, as the home side came more into the game. A spectacular shot from Beckham got the equaliser, and sub Andy Cole wrapped up the points as the nearby Keane and a 55,000 crowd looked on in anticipation. It was United's first title win on home soil in three decades.

Roy Keane got the moment he was waiting for – to lift the Premiership trophy as captain of Manchester United.

Six days later, and the third double in the nineties was on the cards. The Wembley opponents were Newcastle United, desperate to avenge their humiliating 2-0 Wembley defeat at the hands of Arsenal in 1998. The last English team to chase the treble – Liverpool in 1977 – won the league and the European Cup but lost the FA

Cup final to . . . Manchester United. But there were no such slip-ups in '99. As Keane led out his troops on to the Wembley turf, there were no friendly gestures to his opposite number, Alan Shearer, just a resolve to win. Six minutes into the sun-baked game, Keane was tackled by Welsh international Gary Speed. He fell awkwardly and motioned to the bench to come off after ten minutes of pained hobbling. His replacement – striker Teddy Sheringham – made up for a season of few starts with a goal after just ninety seconds. In a one-sided affair, Paul Scholes made it 2-0 in the second half and killed off the Toon Army's dreams.

As he struggled up the Wembley steps, Roy Keane proudly anticipated holding up his second trophy of an unforgettable week. In time-honoured fashion, he shook Prince Charles's hand, kissed the cup and lifted it, to the screams of the Red Army. Walking down those famous steps, with fans begging him to take their scarves, he glanced back in admiration at the man who filled his shoes in the centre of the park, taking the blows and fighting for supremacy. The player? David Beckham.

After the Barcelona triumph which sealed the historic treble, Keane was insistent that the team would not be complacent: 'We won't rest on our laurels. We want to be like the top teams a few years ago, like Liverpool, and come back and win it again. I think that's the sign of a really good team. Please God, we'll be back in the final next year.'

Only God could bet against it.

11

THE LONG ROAD TO GLORY:
MANCHESTER UNITED IN EUROPE 1998-'99

12 August 1998, Old Trafford
Manchester United 2; LKS Lodz 0

Having come second in the Premiership to Arsenal, Manchester United had to qualify for the Champions League. Goals from Ryan Giggs after 15 minutes, and Andy Cole after 80 minutes set up United for the second leg in Poland. Incidentally, eventual finalists Bayern Munich also came second in the Bundesliega.

26 August 1998, LKS Stadium, Poland
LKS Lodz 0; Manchester United 0

Some 400 Reds fans travelled to the dilapidated stadium for this dull draw - but they were still happy to see their team gain a place in the competition proper. Amazingly, the Polish minnows were the only team to stop United scoring in the entire competition, but they were still happy to see their team gain a place in the competition proper.

16 September 1998, Old Trafford
Manchester United 3; FC Barcelona 3

A game that typified Manchester United's season. Win,

lose or draw, United rarely bored spectators over the coming months – and that was so true of this epic encounter, which typified an adrenalin-packed season. The supporters roared on the team, wearing their familiar red and white European strip, as they trooped out on to the Old Trafford turf to the familiar Champions League music, composed by Tony Britten. Captain Roy Keane faced extraordinary players such as the Brazilian Rivaldo in a tension-charged stadium with 53,601 supporters – the biggest attendance anywhere in Europe as the crunch matches began. United were cruising by half-time, after goals from rampant winger Ryan Giggs and ever-dependable scorer Paul Scholes, in the seventeeth and twenty-fourth minutes of the game. But the Catalan giants forced their way back into the thrilling game after the break, with a 47-minute goal from Sonny Anderson, and a disputed penalty by Giovanni (59 minutes) and a Luis Enrique effort (71 minutes). A sixty-third-minute spectacular free kick from David Beckham ensured that United stayed in contention. Still, they were the more disappointed of the two teams after the 3-3 draw.

30 September 1998, Olympiastadion, Munich
Bayern Munich 2; Manchester United 2

Just a fortnight after the Barca clash, United faced an even tougher battle against the uncompromising Germans. The game came just after two tough tests for the Reds – away to Arsenal, which they lost 3-0, and home to Liverpool, where they emerged 2-0 winners. This time Captain Keane faced one of the most physically challenging games of his career. Desperate for European glory were the giants – in every respect – of German football. The Bayern battling midfield included the likes of combative Steffan Effenberg – 6ft 3ins tall and weighing in at 13st 7lb, and Mario Basler, 6ft 1in and almost 13st. Keano, by comparison, is 5ft 11ins and weighs 12st 1lb. The typically well-organised Germans raced into the lead on the eleventh minute with a goal from Giovane Elber, but Dwight Yorke – who was to become joint top-scorer in Europe – pulled one back on the half-hour. Scholes gave United a dream start four minutes into the second half, but the game will forever be remembered for goalkeeper Peter Schmeichel's slip in the ninetieth minute, which gave Bayern the draw that United fans had been dreading. 'Letting the game slip at the death was disappointing and a real kick in the teeth because I felt we were worth a win,' manager Alex Ferguson noted afterwards.

21 October 1998, Parken Stadium, Copenhagen
Brondby IF 2; Manchester United 6

Once more on to the roller coaster with the Red Devils. United were no strangers to Copenhagen, having com-fortably beaten Brondby in a pre-season tour of

Scandinavia. Roy Keane scored his first goal of his impressive European campaign as United recorded the biggest away win in Champions League history. As the Germans played Barcelona at home, and went on to win 1-0 with a Steffan Effenberg goal, United simply had to win this tie. Group minnows they may have been, but Brondby had already shocked Europe with a 2-1 win over Bayern on 30 September. And coach Ebbe Skovdahl, who had witnessed United crushing Wimbledon four days previously, declared he had no fears. United, though, took control of the game almost from kick-off. After being set up with a brilliant pass from young full-back Wesley Brown, Ryan Giggs beat keeper Ruben Bagger in the second minute. Nineteen minutes later, he lashed in another. Andy Cole – who formed a fearsome partnership with new signing Dwight Yorke at home and abroad – whipped in a goal to effectively kill off the tie in the twenty-eighth minute. A goal in the thirty-fifth minute lessened the pain for Skovdahl's team, but then again . . . beware of Roy.

Keano – a massive hero in Scandinavia – scored in the fifty-fifth minute, and it seemed Manchester would run up a cricket score against Peter Schmeichel's former club. Yorke and Solskjaer completed the rout with goals on the hour and then two minutes after, but some pride was restored to many of the 40,315 crowd when local hero Ebbe Sand scored on the ninetieth minute. 'It was football from another planet,' Skovdahl admitted after the match.

4 November 1998, Old Trafford
Manchester United 5; Brondby IF 0

Ebbe Skovdahl joked that United would win by a mile –
and they did. In the first quarter of the game, United
played their best football in the tournament so far and
were cruising at 4-0 up by half-time. Roy Keane orches-
trated the midfield as David Beckham (7 minutes), Andy
Cole (12 minutes), Phil Neville (16 minutes) and Dwight
Yorke (28 minutes) got on the score sheet. In a dull second half, Solksjaer replaced Cole up front while Jordi
Cruyff came on for Ryan Giggs. Paul Scholes gave the
fans the goal they wanted, in the sixty-third minute, but,
ominously, Bayern were to beat Barcelona in front of
100,000 spectators in the daunting Nou Camp. It was an
awesome achievement, as the world's biggest club was in
its centenary year and Barca fans were desperate to make
it to the final, to be staged in their home town.

25 November 1998, Nou Camp, Barcelona
FC Barcelona 3; Manchester United 3

The burden was on Roy Keane as he faced the biggest
game in his entire club career. What resulted was
probably the greatest attacking game ever in the

Champions League. The fiercely passionate Catalans were ecstatic when Sonny Anderson took the lead in the first minute, but United dug in and Dwight Yorke scored after 25 minutes. Keane battled in midfield, and United went ahead in the second half thanks to Andy Cole. The battling Keane, always under the microscope in Europe, got a yellow card. Rivaldo – currently the world's best player – was in breathtaking form, scoring twice to deny United a victory that would give them breathing space in the group. However, Dwight Yorke, also in sparkling form, gave United the draw with a goal in the sixty-eighth minute after some amazing interplay with goalscorer and friend Andy Cole. Only 54,213 fans occupied the Nou Camp, but, even as they went out of the competition, the home fans applauded Manchester United off the pitch after witnessing a stunning match. As UEFA president Lennart Johansson wrote before the 26 May final: 'Whatever the result in Barcelona, Manchester United have made countless friends.'

9 December 1998, Old Trafford
Manchester United 1; Bayern Munich 1

Make-or-break time – yet again. All this only days after gruelling games against title-chasers Leeds United and Aston Villa. Only one team could automatically qualify from the group, and United needed to win to ensure they would go to the top, as they were on eight points, compared with nine for Bayern. In the programme notes, Alex Ferguson noted: 'We lead the entire competition with a tally of 19 goals . . . You might ask questions of our defending at times but nobody can accuse us of being negative or dull!'

United could not afford to slip an early goal, and their defending was the best yet in the competition. Roy Keane dominated German international Jens Jeremies in midfield, while Jaap Stam was a rock in defence. In one of his best European performances to date, Keane, fed the ball by Ryan Giggs, blasted a low and hard shot past keeper Oliver Kahn in the forty-third minute. In the second half, it seemed disaster had struck. Defender Ronny Johnssen had glorious chances to make it 2-0 from corners, but then Hasan Salihamidzic struck for the visitors. The fans needn't have worried. Subs Philip Neville and Teddy Sheringham urged their team-mates to calm down the game, as a draw would now be enough to get United through to the quarter-finals. With ten points, United were home, with NK Croatia Zagreb, Galatasaray, Real Madrid, Lens and PSV Eindhoven all finishing their groups on eight points.

'Perhaps we will meet United again in the later stages,' said Bayern coach Ottmar Hitzfeld.

3 March 1999, Old Trafford
Manchester United 2; Internazionale 0

The pre-match talk was all about the world's top player, Ronaldo, and whether he'd recover in time to threaten United. In the end, United produced the kind of football magic to rank alongside the 3-2 win over Juventus in 1997 or the 4-0 thrashing of Porto in 1996. David Beckham shook hands with Diego Simeone, the man he fouled in the World Cup, resulting in the England player's sending-off. Beckham came of age against Inter, and his crossing was superb, setting up Dwight Yorke with pinpoint accuracy as he scored in the sixth and forty-fifth minutes of the game. But Roy Keane had to be at his very best as Simeone and midfield partner Benoit Cauet attempted to feed balls through to strikers of the calibre of Roberto Baggio and Ivan Zamorano. The latter was substituted for pace, and rising young star Nichola Ventola looked threatening. United were only saved towards the end from conceding a damaging away goal. Defender Henning Berg cleared off the line as the Italians stepped up a gear in the final 20 minutes of the contest.

But by riding their luck at times, United did what Premiership clubs have found impossible – outwitting quality Italian opposition. And it was Italian opposition that had nothing to play for in Serie A, with Lazio and local rivals AC Milan way ahead in the league. However, lady luck was not shining on the dominating presence of Roy Keane, and he got a yellow card for dissent. This put him only one yellow card away from missing the greatest game of his career – the European final.

'We held firm, and defended well at times . . . and Peter Schmeichel made two fantastic saves,' Alex Ferguson said in the post-match press conference. 'Beckham tonight was outstanding – nobody could match him . . . We had all our players fit, and they could not handle Yorke or Beckham, whereas nobody in the Milan team caused us special problems.'

Captain Fantastic Roy Keane vowed not to let the yellow card mellow him on the pitch. 'I am not going to tiptoe around the San Siro not making tackles. I will not hold back. If I do that, it means I have to do it in the semi-final as well.' But he realised the reality of his situation: 'I know all about my yellow card situation, but I can't change now.'

A disappointed Inter coach Mircea Lucescu paid tribute to United, but added, 'We should learn to play from the start of the game and not at the start of the second half, when the damage has been done. We still have a chance in the home leg.'

17 March 1999, San Siro, Milan
Inernazionale 1; Manchester United 1

The Reds clung on for dear life for much of this tense battle in front of 79,528 fans in the intimidating San Siro, one of the great cathedrals of football. Oranges and bottles rained down from the stands on a night of tension, as Inter had their backs against the wall. Roy Keane revealed his anxiety before the epic encounter: 'My caution at Old Trafford was a bit harsh,' and added that he'd watch out for any goading by the opposition: 'I have played against teams like Inter before. The South American players are very similar. You just have to be aware.'

Even before kick-off, it was a case of no prisoners taken. Alex Ferguson was lambasted by the Italian press for attacking their team's gamesmanship, and, as the two sides shook hands on the pitch, Keane ignored Ronaldo – and looked determined to say what he had to on the pitch. He exploded into action straight after the kick-off, executing a one-two with Beckham before whipping in a shot on goal. At the other end, box-to-box Keane headed an important clearance from a Roberto Baggio corner and marshalled his defensive troops against the onslaught. But United looked rattled at times, with Schmeichel tackling striker Ivan Zamorano to the ground and Inter roaring for a penalty.

Time seemed to stand still as Keane, late in the match, tripped Ze Elias. French referee Gilles Veissiere blew his whistle but – to many Reds' relief – awarded a free kick, not a card. The inevitable happened, however – an Inter goal. The pacy rising ace Nicola Ventola came on for unfit Ronaldo, playing despite knee injury worries, and scored after three minutes on the pitch. Keane was at fault, misjudging the fall of the ball in front of goal, and Ventola calmly side-footed it past Schmeichel. United would still go through on aggregate, but fans feared the worst as Internazionale piled on the pressure. Jubilation replaced high anxiety as Paul Scholes coolly steered the ball past top keeper Gianluca Paglicua in the eighty-eighth minute. Bring on Juve!

'For us, this represents a step forward in European football,' said Alex Ferguson. 'To succeed, you have to beat the Italian teams, and we did. In general, I thought we played better than Inter.' But he added: 'I admit we had some lucky moments.' Shocked Inter coach Mircea Lucescu moaned: 'Manchester United are more organised than us, but not better than us. We had some good chances to win and deserved to qualify.' But, he added, 'Now I think Manchester United will reach the final.'

But first, the little matter of getting past Italy's team of the nineties: Juventus.

17 April 1999, Old Trafford
Manchester United 1; Juventus 1

A goal at the death by Ryan Giggs kept United's hopes alive after Juventus scored that all-important away goal. After just 25 minutes, Antonio Conte stunned the 54,487 crowd with the goal the Reds dreaded. Roy Keane was swamped in midfield, and had to contend with two world-class stars – World Cup winner Zinedine Zidane, who put in an excellent performance, despite being below par because of injury, and Dutch hero Edgar Davids. 'We never got going, so I had to get close to Davids and Zidane to stop them from playing.'

In the second half, Juventus took their foot off the pedal and United came more into the action. In wave after wave, the home team pressed forward. The linesman was very late – the decision came 'tomorrow', according to Alex Ferguson – after Paul Scholes looked to have levelled the match, and anxious minutes ticked away. A brilliant Ryan Giggs effort into the top of the net on the ninetieth minute showed United's resilience, but the visitors went home with the advantage of an away goal. 'The late goal gives us a chance in Turin, but it was still a disappointing result from our point of view,' Keane admitted. And he revealed that Juventus were a match for United: 'We did not spot too many weaknesses in their game as they have several world-class players.' French midfielder Didier Deschamps admitted that Juve could have done even better. 'In the first hour, we played well. We are happy with the result and the overall performance but disappointed that we didn't score a second goal.'

Juventus coach Carlo Ancelotti felt his team had 'neutralised both Giggs and Beckham,' but Ferguson maintained, 'I just feel that we are going to win.'

21 April 1999, Stadio delle Alpi, Turin
Juventus 2; Manchester United 3

The night Roy Keane came of age . . . The night he confounded the critics . . . The night he will never forget, much as he may wish to. ABUs from Ireland to Australia, the English fans who had derided Beckham, even followers of arch-rivals Liverpool or Leeds could not grumble about the manner in which United made it to the final.

After just six minutes, Serie A hotshot Filippo Inzhagi got on the end of a Zinedine Zidane corner and shocked the United defence. Five minutes later, he tore through the United defence and his vicious shot deflected off Jaap Stam to beat Schmeichel. United began to look out of their depth; many of the 60,806 crowd roared on Juventus, confident of them appearing in their fourth consecutive final. For a moment, heads dropped, as young stars looked around for leadership. Keane was not prepared to let his European final dream slip so easily. A David Beckham swirling cross was headed past hapless Juventus goalkeeper Angelo Peruzzi by an adrenalin-fuelled Keane.

'We refused to panic,' Denis Irwin recalled after the game. 'We knew we had nearly 80 minutes to get out of trouble, and once Keaney scored, our confidence was in full flow.' Dutch defender Jaap Stam confided, 'I have never played in a team with such self-belief.'

'We were very good for the first 20 minutes and it's difficult to know what happened,' Filipo Inzaghi remembered. 'Suddenly we were pushed back into our own area and they won a corner. From then everything went wrong for us.'

The glory was to last all of eight minutes for the Corkman. A sloppy pass from Jesper Blomqvist forced Keane to tackle Zidane, and it was mis-timed. Although the Frenchman made a meal of a bad challenge, most fans feared the worst. Swiss referee Urs Meier reached for his pocket and pulled out the yellow card that sealed Keane's fate. Win or lose, he would not be in the Champions League final.

What happened next stunned the football world. No tantrums, no tears, no arguing with the referee; just bewilderment, and the realisation that the team needed him. He was to be followed into the book – and out of the final – by Paul Scholes in the second half. Instead of the two goals paving the way for Italian domination, it caused the home side to sit back. Keane and fellow midfield battler Nicky Butt began to get the better of Edgar Davids and Didier Deschamps, with Zidane absent for much of the action. Cole and Yorke combined superbly two minutes after Keano's carding, with Cole putting in a pinpoint cross which was met with a diving header by his pal. 'We gave them too much space. After they made it 2-1, they started to give us problems,' Juve's Carlo Ancelotti admitted.

In the second half, United played the home side off the park, with Cole looking set to beat the keeper ten minutes into the second half, only to miscontrol the ball. At 2-2, United would go through on away goals, and the home side began to leave gaping holes in defence as they pushed forward for that vital strike. The local crowd breathed a sigh of relief when a ferocious Irwin effort clipped the upright.

With minutes to spare, Dwight Yorke and Andy Cole raced away from their markers, only for Yorke to be pulled down in the box by the Juventus keeper. With the ref looking set to award a penalty, Cole sprinted into the area and slotted the loose ball home from an acute angle. Juventus heads dropped, the 4,000 visiting fans went wild and even the home fans managed to applaud the never-say-die winners. 'The finest performance I have ever seen from my team,' said Alex Ferguson.

But Keane and Scholes appeared to be dazed, with the reality not sinking in till long after the game. 'My booking was one of those things,' Roy said about the card, and he faced the situation with courage: 'I knew before the game what a booking would mean. And I think I probably deserved it. It was a bit of a late challenge.' But he went on to say, 'It doesn't really matter because the club has got there.'

Team-mates rallied around the suspended duo. 'Roy will be sorely missed in Barcelona,' said compatriot Denis Irwin. 'He's been outstanding for us all season, a huge influence, especially in big games, and I'm disappointed on a professional, and personal, level.' He also paid tribute to what makes Roy special: 'It was typical of Roy that he didn't let the second yellow card get to him. If anything, it spurred him on. He got us back into the game with a brave header and never stopped driving the team on.'

'I am close friends with both Roy and Paul and their bookings put a dampener on everything,' admitted midfielder Nicky Butt. 'They have been brilliant in the way they played to get us to Barcelona. Now they have paid the ultimate price. It's up to the rest of us to go on and win the trophy for them.' Goal-poacher Dwight Yorke said, 'It's a big loss not to have Roy and Paul available for the final.' Bayern midfield general Steffan Effenberg was disappointed to hear about United's misfortune: 'It's a shame he will miss the final because it would have been a great challenge. I am a great admirer of Keane. He is one of the best midfield players around. He defends well and can also get forward and score, as he showed against us. I enjoyed our battle in the two previous games.' But Effenberg's team-mate Sammy

Kuffour was happier about the news: 'That is good for us. He is such an important player. He holds the midfield together and helps them use so many attacking forces. He is their driving force.'

The cruellest irony was that UEFA had announced that in next year's enlarged competition, players will be suspended only after picking up three yellow cards, not two.

One man who knows well the agony of missing out on a European Cup final is the original king of Old Trafford, Denis Law. The darling of the Stretford End was the team's striker par excellence of the 1960s but missed the Wembley final in 1968 after an injury-ravaged season. 'It was harder for Roy Keane and Paul Scholes because the suspensions only came in the last match, whereas I knew that I wouldn't be playing in the final,' says the affable Scot, who watched the match from his hospital bed. 'But even with two players missing – and they'll miss Roy in particular – they still can bring in other players – that's the beauty of it,' he said before the tie. But he was confident that Roy would get to lift the trophy in his own right. 'Keane's young. I'm sure he'll get another shot at the final.'

26 May 1999, Nou Camp, Barcelona
Manchester United 2; Bayern Munich 1

The world's media assembled in the Nou Camp 24 hours
before kick-off to attend training sessions by finalists
Manchester United and Bayern Munich. Bayern, true to
form, looked disciplined and organised, and reporters
couldn't help but notice their bulk – an average height of
6ft and weight of 12st 12lb. After the Germans left the
field, it was United's turn to go through their paces for
the cameras. The suspended Paul Scholes was in his
tracksuit, and pounded Peter Schmeichel's goal, forcing
the big Dane to pull off some of his trademark incredible
saves. But Roy Keane sat, tracksuited, on the half-way
line, occasionally looking around at the awesome
stadium, somehow devoid of soul without spectators.
Taking a sip from his bottle of water – at 7.45 pm, the
temperature was still high – he was occasionally joined
by reserve keeper Raimond Van Der Gouw or back-up
staff. Alex Ferguson – decked out in a '60s-style United
jersey – came over to Roy, but few words were spoken.
Both men knew the score. At times, the team
looked edgy, as well they might, on the verge of a
history-making treble. In Barcelona's main square, Plaza
De Cataluña, and on the world-famous Las Ramblas, tens

of thousands of Reds were in full voice. 'Keano, Keano' echoed around the proud Catalan capital. It's a tune that has echoed around Old Trafford, Maine Road, Giants Stadium, but never had it sounded so heartfelt.

Wednesday, 26 May, 1999: Manchester United's date with destiny. Two-thirds of the Nou Camp was occupied by the United fans, with English and Irish flags occupying all tiers. The Bayern fans occupied one scoreboard end but made up for smaller numbers with loud chanting and a display of red and white cards which spelled out Bayern's initials, FCB. As 250,000 viewers around the world tuned in, local opera star Montserrat Caballe sang Barcelona to the 90,000 crowd – the biggest ever for a Champions League final. But the game seemed over only minutes after the fat lady had sung. In the sixth minute, Bayern were awarded a free on the edge of the area after Ronny Johnssen brought down giant forward Carsten Jancker. Mario Basler and Steffan Effenberg stood over the ball, and the United defence looked unsure of themselves. Basler lashed a superb free-kick around a badly-positioned Schmeichel, silencing the United faithful. Bayern then closed their game, with their defenders – Lothar Matthaus, Marcus Babbel, Thomas Linke and Samuel Kuffour – snuffing out any threat from Yorke and Cole.

Had the Germans played attacking football, it might have been a different story, but a different United came out all guns blazing after half-time. Ferguson recalled the team talk at the break. 'You just have to find a way to affect people's lives,' he said. 'I told the players, 'This European Cup will be only six feet away from you at the end of this day. But if you lose this match you won't even be able to touch it.' The closest United had come to an equaliser found Jesper Blomqvist one-on-one against keeper Oliver Kahn as a cross came in from Ryan Giggs. The shot cannoned off the Swede's knee, and it looked as if it wasn't going to be Manchester's night. And it could have been all over had it not been for Schmeichel at the other end, who stopped a Steffan Effenberg effort on the hour. Two other German strikes clattered the woodwork, as United desperately raced after the equaliser. Time after time, the massive TV screens in the stadium showed just how close the Germans had come. As the clock ticked away, Sheringham and Solskjaer came on for Cole and Blomqvist. FA Cup hero Sheringham, in particular, was gunning for the Germans. 'Just as Basler was waiting to take a corner with Bayern leading 1-0, he was waving to his fans. I was stood right next to him warming up – and I couldn't believe what was going on. That sort of behaviour gives you a great incentive to score a goal,' he recalled. Twenty minutes later, it was injury time, and the Bayern fans were in seventh heaven, their players only hanging on till the final whistle. Hanging on for European glory. And then, a sort of slow motion that will be remembered by millions. 'Time was up and I looked around and saw the cup was on its way down, with the Bayern colours draped on it,' said Beckham. Already, UEFA president Lennart Johansson, flanked by security guards, had left his seat and taken the lift down to the pitch to present the cup to Bayern.

Ninety minutes on the clock . . . game all but over. Super-sub Teddy Sheringham has been making a habit of breaking hearts – Geordie hearts with his FA Cup goal four days previously, and now he was to repeat the feat.

The Germans seemed rattled as the bulky presence of Peter Schmeichel came up for the corner. Three men jumped with him, for the ball to bounce away. Yorke nodded it back into the danger area, defender Thomas Linke mis-kicked, Giggsy pounced and the ball was turned in by Teddy Sheringham.

The ground erupted, as if an earthquake had just hit Catalonia. Red flares soared up into the night sky, and the stadium began to heave with waves of bodies. The Bayern players sank to the ground, seemingly exhausted. But the script was to get worse for the team dubbed FC Hollywood. Less than two minutes later, with TV companies still showing the replay of the goal, Beckham lined up a late, late corner. Keeper Kahn pushed his own defenders out of his path, and sub Ole Gunnar Solskjaer had the room he needed to blast the ball into the top of the net. Even in celebration, the United fans could not quite believe what they were seeing, this re-run of the last-gasp Ole goal against Liverpool in the FA Cup. Johanssen's lift arrived at the ground floor as the 'losers' danced around in celebration and the would-be winners collapsed on to the turf, distraught, not comprehending how their team had snatched defeat from the jaws of victory. It was the greatest escape from German opposition since the days of Steve McQueen and Co.

Gary Neville rolled around the ground, hugging team-mates; Peter Schmeichel bounced around the pitch in some form of tribal dance; Teddy Sheringham's smile was even wider than Dwight Yorke's trademark grin; the stadium tannoy blasted out the calypso and the tune to 'You are my Sunshine', to which the United fans sang 'You are my Solskjaer.'

Roy Keane and Paul Scholes walked on to the pitch, looking uncomfortable in their designer suits rather than the Champions League strip. Keano waved to the masses of United fans behind the German keeper's goal and was hugged by Andy Cole and Ryan Giggs. He looked out of place, but he was not forgotten by the team. After the cup was lifted – the roar would have lifted off any roof, he and Scholesy were urged back on to the pitch by the fans, and by the players. A guard of honour was formed at the tunnel, and the crowd cheered on the heroes of the previous matches, the men who had helped make this magical night possible. And the biggest cheer was reserved for Keane, as he lifted the trophy and showed it off to the world.

After the exhilaration, the media packed out the tunnel below, waiting for the heroes to make an appearance on the way to the team bus. The silent Bayern players filed past, eager to get away, and club president Franz Beckenbauer had a terse 'good night' for the throng. A beaming David Beckham spoke for the cameras, nonchalantly carrying the cup by his side. All in a day's work – he looked completely at ease.

Alex Ferguson recalled that the date would have been United legend Sir Matt Busby's ninetieth birthday. 'I think he was praying for us tonight,' he said with a smile.

Last out was Roy Keane, who tried to remain upbeat and composed. 'It's not the same, is it, sitting in the stand with a match like that going on. But we had to play 12 or 13 games to get here and I was involved,' he said. 'I got a medal too – when one of the lads was in the shower, I nicked it,' he joked. But he told the media, 'Christ, it's been a frustrating week, of course it has.' And referring to the guard of honour, the level-headed player said, 'I didn't really want it, but it's nice, even if it's a little bit embarrassing.'

And he concluded that, 'If we'd lost together we would have consoled each other, but tonight we're going to party together.'